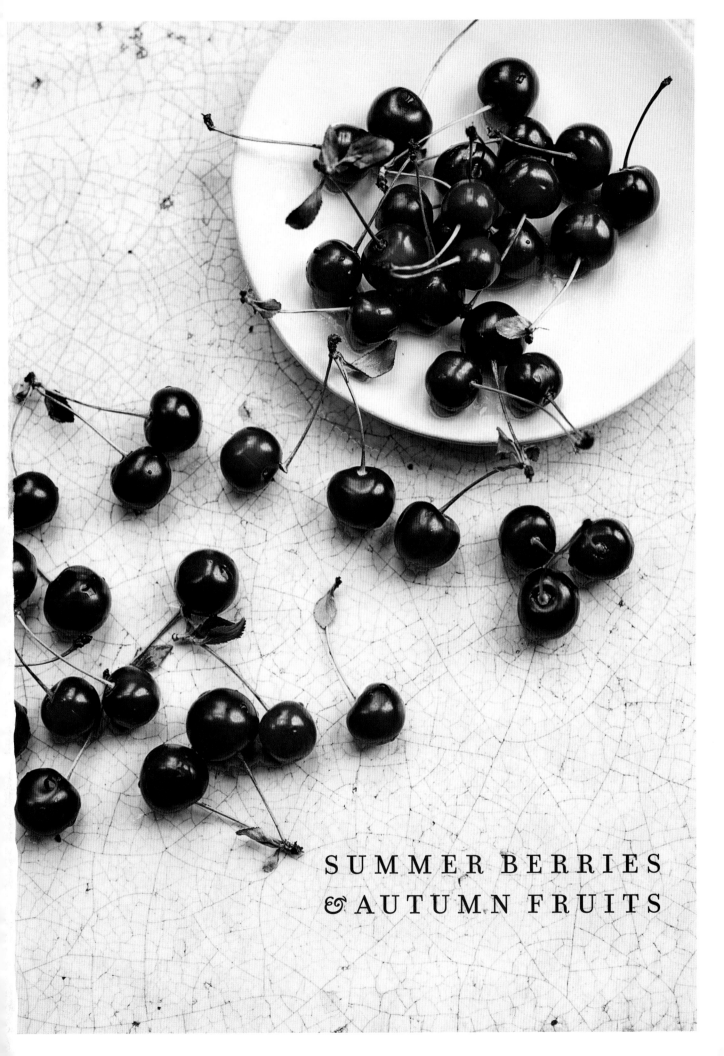

SUMMER BERRIES
& AUTUMN FRUITS

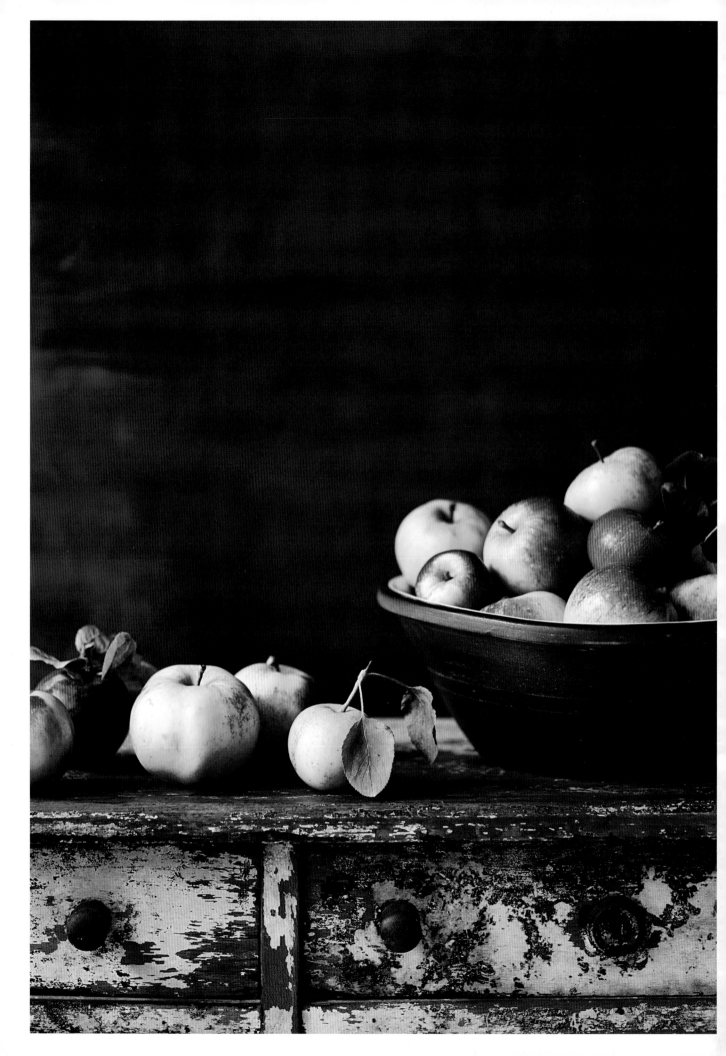

Annie Rigg

SUMMER BERRIES & AUTUMN FRUITS

120 sensational sweet & savoury recipes

PHOTOGRAPHY BY TARA FISHER

KYLE BOOKS

To my Mother who finds it impossible
to make just one pudding *x*

First published in Great Britain in 2015 by Kyle Books,
an imprint of Kyle Cathie Ltd
192-198 Vauxhall Bridge Road
London SW1V 1DX
general.enquiries@kylebooks.com
www.kylebooks.com

10 9 8 7 6 5 4 3 2 1

ISBN 978 0 85783 255 9

Editor: Judith Hannam
Copy Editor: Jo Richardson
Designer: Miranda Harvey
Photographer: Tara Fisher
Food and Prop Stylist: Annie Rigg
Production: Nic Jones and Gemma John

A Cataloguing in Publication record for this title is
available from the British Library.

Colour reproduction by ALTA London.
Printed and bound in China by 1010 International
Printing Ltd.

Contents

Introduction

Throughout the days, weeks and months of writing this book my kitchen has been a joy and filled with a constantly changing and seasonal spread of the best available fruit from gardens, farmers markets, specialist suppliers and growers. And just when I think I've overloaded on one type of fruit along comes another – overlapping in a way that revitalises my mind, body and cooking. Although this book isn't necessarily season specific, it's impossible to ignore the fact that fruit (or any produce for that matter) eaten at optimum ripeness and harvested or picked at it's peak is not only better for you, it tastes far superior and is often cheaper. If you are lucky and green fingered enough to grown your own produce, either in your garden or allotment, then you'll appreciate the thrill of walking to the end of the garden, trug or basket in hand, to select the best of the days offerings – still warm from the sunshine or glistening in rain drops.

In the depths of Winter, when almost all of our native fruits in the UK are still a way off, I am glad for the cheering bowl of citrus fruits that greets me in the morning when I venture into the kitchen. Lip puckering grapefruits and oranges both regular and blood, or smaller varieties such as juicy clementines and mandarins provide a much needed hit of vitamin C to boost the immune system and help keep colds at bay. A large bowl of mixed citrus fruit, cut into neat segments and perhaps adorned with some pomegranate seeds, passion fruit or blueberries is just the kind of breakfast that one needs on darker days.

As Spring comes knocking my thoughts turn to rhubarb – starting with the almost neon pink forced varieties which also makes a fantastic breakfast when lightly stewed and served with natural yoghurt and a good scattering of granola (homemade if you're of that persuasion). What follows is a profusion of berries with enough variation to keep even the most jaded cook happy. There's preserving to be done, ice cream and sorbets to be made and light summery cakes and desserts aplenty. On the whole, I prefer to reserve berries for use in sweet cooking but late summer raspberries and blackberries work well with grouse and other early game.

To spoil us further in the balmy summer months we are blessed with stone fruits; cherries in colours from blushing pink and yellow to red and deep purple, apricots, plums, greengages, damsons and peaches and nectarines with their downy skin. Peaches are possibly one of my favourite fruits, both yellow and white fleshed, round or flat shaped and churned into ice cream, baked into a pie or sliced and served alongside rich, creamy buffalo mozzarella – or simply eaten in the hand with juice dripping down my chin. And I'm not sure anyone can resist a paper bag full of juicy deep red cherries – always buy double the amount you need for cooking a particular recipe as you'll start eating them before you get home, guaranteed.

Orchard fruits now have a greater significance in my cooking as we have a selection of apple and pear trees in our garden. With my plans to add quince and plum to the mix I'll be finding inventive ways to use what I hope will be a plentiful harvest each autumn. I'm sure that I'll be able to find willing tasters for my apple caramels, and apple pies never fail to please, but I also have an apple press on my wish list for making homemade cider and juice which will no doubt make the most of what can't be cooked with, eaten or given away.

Throughout the year brightly coloured tropical fruit is in constant supply. Mangoes are grown from South America to India, South East Asia and beyond and vary in size, shape and sweetness. They have thousands of uses and can be diced into salsa and salads, whizzed into smoothies, lassis and cocktails. Many tropical fruits pair well with searing hot chillies, salty dressings and fresh herbs in salads and sauces – the cooling sweetness of the fruit tempering the chilli's bite. Melons are plentiful in the European summer months as any market in France, Italy or Spain will demonstrate, and what could be nicer than a plate of wafer-thin slices of salty Parma ham served alongside juicy melon wedges on a hot summer day?

This book is a collection of recipes that reflect the way I like to cook and eat, using fruits that are widely available rather than the obscure and unusual. Within these pages are recipes for preserving including marmalades, jams, curds and pickles and I have included recipes for drinks – both alcoholic and otherwise. Peach shrub is new discovery and a recipe that can be adapted to suit other fruits such as berries, apricots and plums, and although refreshing diluted with soda water as a long drink it can be added to your cocktail experiments, perhaps with a dash of bourbon and ginger ale. In each chapter you'll find a wide selection of baking ideas, from crisp wafer biscuits for serving with cheese and cakes laden with berries to soufflés, pies, tarts and doughnuts. The book is divided into five chapters of fruit varieties and each chapter contains recipes for both sweet and savoury dishes which really only scratch the surface of this wonderfully inspiring subject. I wish this book had been four times as long!

I'd like to point out a few notes on commonly used ingredients in my recipes. When using eggs always use the size stated in a recipe and organic or free range as a matter of principle. I tend to use sea salt flakes (such as Maldon) as I feel that this gives a better flavour than regular table salt. I always recommend that you use unsalted butter, particularly for baking, and add salt to taste. With other dry ingredients such as flour, sugar and chocolate I use the best available or to fit my budget. Dried fruit and nuts should be fresh – which sounds like a contradiction but nuts do have a tendency to turn rancid if well past the use-by dates.

As I write these words Seville oranges have just started to make an appearance in the shops and I am looking forward to a weekend of marmalade making. Grapefruits are at their juicy best and blood oranges are hot on their heels. I'm already eagerly anticipating what the coming months have to offer from the garden, orchard and fruit farm.

Citrus

A ray of sunshine in the dark months of a northern European winter, a bowl of citrus fruit brings joy to my kitchen and cooking. From leafy little mandarins and clementines to sweet, juicy blood oranges and grapefruit in colours ranging from the palest yellow to nearly crimson – barely a day goes by without me either eating or cooking with citrus fruit in one way or another.

I am constantly dazzled by the variety of dishes that can be created from citrus fruit. They are surely the most varied and versatile of all the fruits, the skin, juice and flesh all having a myriad of uses with almost nothing going to waste. From preserves, pickles and drinks to cakes and bakes through to salads, sauces and dressings, and taking inspiration from all corners of the globe, this subject is worthy of a book all of its own.

I always eat fruit for breakfast and when grapefruits are plentiful during the winter months I can't get enough of them. Skin and segment a mixture of white, pink and ruby grapefruits and perhaps a couple of blood or regular oranges and add a handful of blueberries, passion fruit or pomegranate seeds. This breakfast is a real wake-up call for the senses.

The start of the short Seville orange season in January is eagerly awaited by cooks like myself, who snaffle bags of the wrinkly, slightly gnarly fruits whenever they see them. Thick-skinned, loaded with pips and not overly pleasant to eat raw, their bitterness and high pectin content are perfect for marmalade making. Blood oranges also have a short season and were originally grown in Italy, Sicily and Spain. Depending on variety, they are sweeter than normal oranges with a flesh and skin that range in colour from being lightly tinged with a pink blush to the Moro variety, that towards the end of the season can have an almost burgundy-coloured flesh. They can be used whenever a recipe calls for regular oranges but are especially wonderful in simple jellies, dressings or juices, where their distinct flavour and colour really shine.

Bergamot is another short-seasoned fruit and one that is gaining in popularity and availability. With their pale yellow-coloured flesh, not dissimilar to a lemon, these fruits pack a punch with a highly fragrant scent that provides Earl Grey tea with its distinct perfume and make a wonderful syrup or palate-cleansing sorbet.

If a recipe calls for only the juice of an orange or lemon, remove the peels with a vegetable peeler and either slip them into a jar of caster sugar to make scented sugar or dry on a baking tray in a low oven and store in an airtight jar. Two or three strips used in a stew will give it a deeply aromatic citrus note. Or you could make my Orange Bitters on page 14. If you only need half a lemon, slice the remainder, store in a bag in the freezer and slip a frozen slice or two into a G&T.

When grating zest, always grate the fruit directly over the bowl or pan that you are using to catch any precious oils that are released from the skin. Citrus juice provides an acidic balancing note to dishes, instantly bringing food to life – a squeeze of lemon or lime juice can transform a salad or simple grilled meats and fish.

Bergamot and Mandarin Mini Financiers

The bergamot season is relatively short, so, as with Sevilles, you need to snap them up when you see them. Bergamots can vary in size and colour from that of a small lemon to a large orange, and from yellow to pale green and almost orange, but the moment you press the oils from the skin and breathe in the scent, you'll be certain of what's inside. Bergamots are used to flavour Earl Grey tea and this marmalade variation has the same intense perfume. Tiny delicate morsels such as these seem almost innocent due to their size, but these little cakes pack a punch flavour-wise. If you can't find bergamots, or they are out of season, simply use a large lemon.

MAKES 36 MINI MUFFIN-SIZED CAKES

75G PLAIN FLOUR, PLUS EXTRA FOR DUSTING

125G GROUND ALMONDS

150G ICING SUGAR

¼ TEASPOON BAKING POWDER

125G UNSALTED BUTTER, DICED, PLUS EXTRA, MELTED, FOR GREASING

1 TABLESPOON CLEAR FRAGRANT HONEY

FINELY GRATED ZEST OF 1 BERGAMOT

FINELY GRATED ZEST OF 1 MANDARIN

3 LARGE EGG WHITES

A PINCH OF FINE SEA SALT

For the bergamot syrup

JUICE OF 1 BERGAMOT

JUICE OF 2 MANDARINS

4 TABLESPOONS CASTER SUGAR

Equipment

2–3 x 12-HOLE MINI MUFFIN TINS OR 12-HOLE MUFFIN TIN

Preheat the oven to 180°C/gas mark 4. Lightly grease the muffin tins with melted butter and dust with a little flour, tapping out the excess.

Sift the flour, ground almonds, icing sugar and baking powder onto a sheet of baking parchment.

Melt the butter in a small saucepan over a low heat, then cook for a couple of minutes until it starts to smell nutty and turns a deep golden brown, swirling the pan to ensure that it browns evenly. Pour into a bowl, add the honey and zests and leave to cool slightly.

In a separate bowl, whisk the egg whites with the salt until they will hold soft peaks. Add the sifted dry ingredients and fold in using a large metal spoon. Pour the melted butter around the edge of the bowl and carefully fold into the batter, being careful not to knock out too much air. Fill three-quarters of each muffin tin hole and bake on the middle shelf of the oven for 10 minutes until well risen and golden brown.

Meanwhile, combine all the syrup ingredients plus 5 tablespoons of water in a small saucepan and set over a low heat to dissolve the sugar. Bring to a gentle simmer and cook until reduced by half.

Leave the cakes to cool in the tins for 2 minutes, then turn out onto a wire rack. Brush the warm cakes with the syrup and leave until cold.

Orange Bitters

Bitters are a wonderful way to add a retro twist to your cocktail making and are firmly back in fashion with the cocktail cognoscenti. Although easy to make at home, you will need to invest in some high-proof vodka, available online or from specialist spirit suppliers, and allow a few weeks for the orange and spices to infuse the spirit. This almost pure vodka is definitely not intended as a mixing vodka and should only be used in small quantities and with caution – in this case, a little really does go a long way. If you are making bitters when Seville oranges are in season, do use them in this recipe, but regular oranges will do.

MAKES 500ML

4 FIRM ORANGES, SCRUBBED IN SOAPY WATER AND DRIED

500ML 88%-BY-VOLUME VODKA (176° PROOF)

1 LARGE CINNAMON STICK, SNAPPED IN HALF

½ VANILLA POD

6 GREEN CARDAMOM PODS

1 TEASPOON BLACK PEPPERCORNS

1 TEASPOON FENNEL SEEDS

1 TEASPOON CORIANDER SEEDS

Equipment

LARGE JAR WITH A TIGHT-FITTING LID

COFFEE FILTER PAPERS OR
CLEAN FINE MUSLIN

SELECTION OF SMALL BOTTLES

Preheat the oven to 120°C/gas mark ½. Remove the peel of each orange using a vegetable peeler – you're after long, thin strips with as little pith as possible. Line a baking tray with baking parchment and scatter the peel strips on top in a single layer. Place in the oven for 45 minutes–1 hour until dry but not browned.

Pour the vodka into the large jar and add the dried peels, cinnamon halves and vanilla pod. Using a pestle and mortar, bruise the cardamom pods to break the skins, then add the other whole spices and give them a light bashing, just enough to break them in half. Add to the vodka, screw the lid on tightly and give the whole lot a good shake to muddle the flavours.

Leave the jar in a cool, dark spot for 2 weeks but preferably at least 4, and shake the jar once a day. After a couple of days the orange peels will have begun to impart a wonderful glow to the vodka.

Strain the vodka through either a coffee filter paper or clean fine muslin into a jug. Pour into clean small bottles and get creative with cocktails.

Add a drop of orange bitters to a Martini or Champagne cocktail,
or use to pep up a G&T. Or decant into small bottles to give as gifts
to the cocktail enthusiast in your life – just add a note of caution
regarding the alcohol content!

Chocolate Orange Delice

This is a pulling-out-all-the-stops type of recipe – one that takes a little time and requires some skill, but it gives back in terms of impact. Think grown-up, fancy pants Jaffa Cakes.

While I appreciate that this recipe might seem long, in reality it's two for the price of one. You can make it as I suggest or, if you only want petit fours, you could just make the orange *pâte de fruit*. Follow the instructions for that part, pour into a smaller tin (a lined 450g loaf tin would work well), leave overnight to set firm, then cut the *pâte* into shapes and toss in granulated or caster sugar, or dip in melted dark chocolate for a sophisticated spin.

For this recipe I suggest using a chocolate of 68–70% cocoa solids. This is my personal preference, and I think it gives a nice balance to the bitter orange, but if your taste is either for something sweeter or more bitter, feel free to use a lower or higher percentage.

SERVES 10–12

For the cake

75G UNSALTED BUTTER, SOFTENED, PLUS
EXTRA FOR GREASING

40G CASTER SUGAR

25G ICING SUGAR

1 MEDIUM EGG, BEATEN

¼ TEASPOON ALMOND EXTRACT

40G PLAIN FLOUR

¼ TEASPOON BAKING POWDER

30G GROUND ALMONDS

A PINCH OF SALT

1 DESSERTSPOON MILK

75G DARK CHOCOLATE, MELTED

For the pâte de fruit layer

3 ORANGES

4 MANDARINS

300G CASTER SUGAR

60G APPLE-BASED LIQUID PECTIN
(CERTO BRAND)

2 TEASPOONS LEMON JUICE

Continued overleaf...

Start by making the cake. Preheat the oven to 170°C/gas mark 3. Grease and line the tin with baking parchment. Cream the butter with both sugars until light and fluffy. Gradually add the beaten egg, a little at a time, beating well between additions and scraping down the sides of the bowl with a rubber spatula. Add the almond extract and mix again. Sift the dry ingredients into the bowl, add the milk and mix again until smooth. Spoon into the prepared tin, level and bake on the middle shelf of the oven for 9–10 minutes, or until pale golden and a wooden skewer comes out clean when inserted into the middle of the cake. Leave to cool in the tin for 2–3 minutes, then, using the baking parchment, carefully lift out onto a wire rack and leave until completely cold. Wash the tin, then line the base and sides with a sheet of clingfilm.

Spread the melted chocolate evenly over the top of the cake and leave to set. Carefully flip the cake back into the lined tin so that the chocolate is now on the underside.

To make the *pâte de fruit* layer, scrub one orange and two mandarins in hot, soapy water to remove any wax or dirt. Place in a saucepan, cover with cold water and bring to the boil, then simmer gently for 15 minutes until the skins are softened. Drain and leave to cool for a few minutes.

Cut a thin slice off the top of the softened fruit to remove the stalk end and discard. Cut the fruit into quarters and cut out any seeds and the central pithy core. Roughly chop the quartered fruit, tip into a food processor and whizz until nearly smooth. Push the pulp through a sieve and weigh the resulting purée – you will need about 200g. Squeeze the juice from the remaining fruit – you will need 350ml.

For the ganache

250ML WHIPPING CREAM

40G LIGHT MUSCOVADO SUGAR

A PINCH OF SALT

225G DARK CHOCOLATE, FINELY CHOPPED

50G UNSALTED BUTTER AT ROOM TEMPERATURE, DICED

For the glaze

100G DARK CHOCOLATE, FINELY CHOPPED

45G UNSALTED BUTTER

40G FULL-FAT MILK

15G CLEAR HONEY

2 TABLESPOONS COCOA POWDER

Equipment

20CM SQUARE CAKE TIN

SUGAR THERMOMETER

Tip half the sugar into a medium saucepan and add 2–3 tablespoons of water. Set over a low heat and dissolve the sugar without stirring. Bring the syrup to the boil and cook until it becomes a deep amber-coloured caramel. Off the heat, slowly and carefully add the juice, purée and remaining sugar. Stir until smooth, then return to a low heat to dissolve any hardened caramel. Pop a sugar thermometer into the pan, bring to a steady gentle simmer and cook until the mixture reaches 107°C. Add the pectin and lemon juice, whisk to combine, then cook until the mixture again reaches 107°C, stirring from time to time. Simmer at this temperature for 2 minutes, stirring frequently. Drop ½ teaspoon of the mixture onto a chilled saucer and leave for about 30 seconds – it should wrinkle when pushed with the tip of your finger. If not, cook for a further minute and test again. Slide the pan off the heat and remove the thermometer. Wait for the bubbling to subside, then pour on top of the cake. Leave for at least 2 hours until cold and set firm.

To make the ganache, in a small saucepan, bring the cream to the boil with the sugar and salt. Immediately remove from the heat and pour over the chocolate in a bowl. Mix until smooth and shiny before adding the butter and beating to combine. Pour over the set *pâte de fruit*, spread level with a palette knife and leave somewhere cool until set firm.

To make the glaze, melt the chocolate and butter with the milk and honey in a small saucepan over a low heat, stirring until smooth. Cool for 3 minutes or so before pouring over the ganache. Tap the tin on the work surface to spread level and leave until set before dusting with the cocoa.

To serve, cut into thin slices using a warmed, long-bladed knife.

Blood Orange Granita

A wonderfully refreshing frozen dessert that doesn't require any great skill or an ice-cream maker, granita is the rough, gritty cousin of smooth sorbet or unctuous ice cream.

SERVES 6

225G CASTER SUGAR

8–10 BLOOD ORANGES, TO YIELD
550–600ML JUICE

JUICE OF ½ LEMON

2 TABLESPOONS CAMPARI, PLUS EXTRA
FOR DRIZZLING (BOTH OPTIONAL)

Equipment
LARGE PLASTIC FREEZER BOX

Tip the caster sugar into a medium saucepan, add 250ml of cold water and bring to the boil. Simmer for 2 minutes, then remove from the heat and leave to cool to room temperature.

Mix together the orange and lemon juices, and the Campari, if using. Add the sugar syrup and whisk to combine. Pour into the freezer box and freeze for 2–3 hours, ensuring it is sitting level. Remove from the freezer and, using a fork, scrape any ice crystals that have formed around the edges of the mixture back into the middle, but do not over-mix – you want large crystals or fine shards. Freeze for a further 2 hours and fork the crystals back again. When the whole mixture has frozen, use the fork to scrape the frozen orange syrup into fine, icy shards – it may well double in volume.

Keep frozen until ready to serve, piled into mounds in chilled bowls with perhaps an extra drizzle of Campari.

Bergamot Syrup

Bergamots (sometimes called sweet lemons or bergamotto) are the ugly sisters of the citrus world, with wrinkles and gnarls and an uneven skin tone. But cut one open and they turn into Cinderella. The smell is almost overwhelmingly citrus but with sweet, perfumed undertones, though the juice can be alarmingly bitter and sharp.

This syrup is delicious added to a glass of prosecco or cava for a citrus twist on a kir royale, but can also be made into a rather special sorbet. Simply add the juice of a lemon to half of the syrup and dilute to taste with about 500ml cold water, then churn in an ice-cream maker according to the manufacturer's instructions.

MAKES ABOUT 1 LITRE

6 BERGAMOTS, SCRUBBED IN HOT,
SOAPY WATER AND DRIED

500G CASTER SUGAR

1 BAY LEAF

2 STAR ANISE

Remove the bergamot zest using the fine side of a grater or preferably a Microplane grater if you have one. Cut the fruits in half and press through a juicer – you should aim to have about 300ml of juice but a little over or under is fine.

Tip the zest into a saucepan with the sugar, bay leaf, star anise and 500ml of cold water and bring slowly to the boil. Simmer gently for 2–3 minutes until slightly thickened and then add the juice. Bring back to a simmer and cook for a further 2 minutes. Remove from the heat and leave to cool to room temperature .

Caramelised Mandarin Salad

When we were young, my mother's culinary repertoire for more fancy occasions included a dessert of caramelised oranges, served more often than not with a pile of creamed-filled brandy snaps alongside – a true 1970s classic. The oranges were sliced and lay in slightly bitter caramel juice, with crisp caramel shards on top – whether by design or not I was never sure. This is my updated, lighter and more refreshing version, which wouldn't look out of place on a festive Christmas table. With or without the brandy snaps.

SERVES 4–6

8-10 MANDARINS OR CLEMENTINES – CHOOSE FIRM ONES, WHICH ARE EASIER TO PEEL

100G CASTER SUGAR

JUICE OF 2 LARGE ORANGES

1–2 TEASPOONS ROSEWATER OR ORANGE FLOWER WATER

SEEDS FROM ½ POMEGRANATE

50G SHELLED PISTACHIOS, ROUGHLY CHOPPED

2–3 SPRIGS OF MINT, ROUGHLY CHOPPED

For a more elegant look to the finished salad, rather than using your hands to peel the mandarins, cut a thin slice off the top and bottom of each and sit them upright on the chopping board. Using a sharp, serrated knife, and working from top to bottom, cut the peel away in strips using a sawing action. Try to cut all of the pith away, leaving the fruit in a neat barrel shape. Cut each mandarin in half through the middle and arrange in a serving dish.

To make the caramel, tip the sugar into a heavy-bottomed saucepan, add 2 tablespoons of cold water and set over a low–medium heat to dissolve the sugar without stirring. Raise the heat to medium, bring the syrup to the boil and cook until it becomes amber-coloured, swirling the pan to ensure that it cooks evenly.

Meanwhile, heat the orange juice until just below boiling in a separate saucepan or in a jug in the microwave. Slide the caramel pan off the heat and carefully add the hot juice – the caramel will splutter furiously, so keep your hands covered by a cloth and your face away from the pan. Return to the heat to melt any hardened caramel, bring to the boil and simmer for 1 minute. Remove from the heat, add the rosewater or orange flower water and leave to cool for a few minutes.

Pour the caramel over the mandarins and stir gently to coat the fruit. Leave for 1 hour or so for the caramel to flavour the little oranges and vice versa.

Scatter over the pomegranate seeds, pistachios and mint and serve.

Cured Citrus Salmon

As the fish is cured rather than cooked or smoked in this recipe, you will need to source some sparkly, spanking fresh salmon for the best results.

This is an ideal dish to serve as a dinner party starter or at a festive meal, as it requires no last-minute cooking or fiddling around. Serve with a simple salad of lightly pickled cucumber and radishes and perhaps some rye or pumpernickel bread.

SERVES 8

1 LARGE ORANGE

2 LIMES

1 UNWAXED LEMON

3 TABLESPOONS SEA SALT FLAKES, SUCH AS MALDON

2 TABLESPOONS GOLDEN CASTER SUGAR

1 TEASPOON JUNIPER BERRIES

1 TEASPOON BLACK PEPPERCORNS

1 TEASPOON FENNEL SEEDS

½ TEASPOON CORIANDER SEEDS

1 STAR ANISE

4 TABLESPOONS FINELY CHOPPED DILL

1 WHOLE FILLETED SIDE OF SALMON, SKIN ON, WEIGHING ABOUT 1KG, SCALED AND PIN-BONED

Equipment

2 LARGE, SHALLOW BAKING TINS OR TRAYS

BAG OF FLOUR OR SUGAR, OR A COUPLE OF FOOD CANS, AS WEIGHTS

Cover one tin or tray with a triple thickness of clingfilm, leaving plenty of excess draping over the sides for wrapping the salmon later.

Wash and dry the citrus fruits and finely grate the zests – if you have a Microplane grater, now is the time to put it to good use. Mix the grated zests with the sea salt flakes and sugar. Lightly crush the juniper berries, peppercorns and fennel and coriander seeds using a pestle and mortar and add to the salt mix. Break the star anise into small pieces and coarsely grind, then add to the salt mixture with half the chopped dill and mix well.

Scatter one-third of the salt mixture over the middle of the clingfilm-covered tin. Lay the salmon on top, skin-side down, and cover with the remaining salt mixture, pressing it into the fish with your hands. Tightly wrap the salmon in the clingfilm and cover with the second tin or tray topped with weighty food items. Leave the salmon to cure in the fridge for 48 hours.

Unwrap the salmon, scrape off as much of the salt as you can and pat dry with kitchen paper. Scatter the salmon with the remaining chopped dill and cut into thin slices with a sharp knife.

Fromage Frais Panna Cotta with Blood Orange Jelly

Jelly and cream. It's a combination that instantly brings to mind children's parties – with little fancy shaped jellies in brightly coloured paper bowls sitting in a lake of cream or ice cream. This version, however, is more suited to adults. The contrast between refreshing blood orange jelly and the cool, slightly tangy panna cotta not only looks rather beautiful but is quite delicious too, especially when served with the Orange and Anise Biscotti on page 29.

SERVES 8

For the jelly

3 LEAVES OF PLATINUM-GRADE
LEAF GELATINE

ABOUT 8 BLOOD ORANGES,
TO YIELD 500ML JUICE

2 TABLESPOONS CASTER SUGAR, OR TO TASTE

For the panna cotta

½ VANILLA POD (OR 1 TEASPOON VANILLA
BEAN PASTE)

350ML DOUBLE CREAM

75G CASTER SUGAR

1 STRIP OF PEEL FROM AN UNWAXED LEMON

4 LEAVES OF PLATINUM-GRADE
LEAF GELATINE

550G FROMAGE FRAIS

Start by making the jelly. Soak the gelatine leaves in a bowl of cold water for 10 minutes to soften. In a small saucepan, bring 100ml of the orange juice and the sugar to just below boiling point over a medium heat. Stir to dissolve the sugar, then remove from the heat. Drain the gelatine and squeeze out any excess water – I also like to blot it quickly on a clean tea towel or kitchen paper. Add to the hot juice and whisk until it has melted. Pour into a jug, add the remaining orange juice and whisk again. Taste for sweetness, adding a little more sugar if needed. Divide the jelly between eight glasses, arrange on a tray and slide into the fridge to chill and set firm – this will take at least 2 hours.

Now make the panna cotta. If using the vanilla pod, slit it down its length with the point of a sharp knife and scrape the seeds into a small saucepan, then add the empty pod to the pan (or just add the vanilla paste). Add the cream, sugar and lemon peel and bring slowly to just below boiling point, then remove from the heat and leave for 20 minutes to infuse. Meanwhile, soak the gelatine leaves in a bowl of cold water for about 10 minutes to soften.

Return the infused cream to just below boiling point. Drain the gelatine and quickly blot dry before whisking into the cream. Add the fromage frais and whisk until smooth, then strain into a jug. Leave to cool slightly, then carefully pour over the set jelly. Cover the glasses with clingfilm and leave in the fridge for about 4 hours or until set.

Orange and Anise Biscotti

I'm rather keen on these elegant, wafer-thin biscotti, which almost melt in the mouth and are ideal to serve alongside creamy desserts, sorbets or simply with vin santo and/or coffee. The uncooked mixture is softer than one would expect for biscotti, hence the need to bake it in a loaf tin rather than free-form, as is usual.

MAKES ABOUT 60

BUTTER, FOR GREASING

150G BLANCHED ALMONDS

4 LARGE EGGS

250G CASTER SUGAR

FINELY GRATED ZEST OF 1 LARGE ORANGE

1 TEASPOON VANILLA EXTRACT

1–2 TEASPOONS LIGHTLY CRUSHED ANISE SEEDS

375G PLAIN FLOUR

1 TEASPOON BAKING POWDER

½ TEASPOON BICARBONATE OF SODA

A GOOD PINCH OF SEA SALT FLAKES

Equipment

2 x 900G LOAF TINS

Preheat the oven to 170°C/gas mark 3. Grease and line the base and sides of the loaf tins with baking parchment.

Tip the almonds onto a baking tray and lightly toast in the oven for 4 minutes until pale golden. Cool and roughly chop.

Whisk the eggs with the sugar for 2–3 minutes until light and foamy. Add the orange zest, vanilla and anise and whisk to combine. Sift the flour, baking powder, bicarbonate of soda and salt into the bowl, add the toasted almonds and combine.

Divide the dough in half, spoon into the prepared tins, spread level and bake on the middle shelf of the oven for about 30 minutes until risen, firm and golden. Leave to cool in the tins for 10 minutes, then turn out onto a wire rack and leave until completely cold. Reduce the oven temperature to 150°C/gas mark 2.

Using a long, serrated bread knife, cut each loaf into slices no thicker than 2mm and arrange on baking parchment-covered baking trays. Bake in batches on the middle shelf for 15–20 minutes until crisp and very lightly toasted, swapping the trays around so that they cook evenly. Remove and cool on wire racks before serving. They will keep for up to 1 week in an airtight box.

Lemon and Poppy Seed Madeleines

This is a multi-cultural bake if ever there was one, with a nod to France from whence the buttery madeleine originated, a wink to the USA and Eastern Europe for the addition of poppy seeds and a cheeky grin to Great Britain for the nifty use of lemon curd. Madeleine tins can vary in size and shape, so the number of cakes that you'll get from this recipe will vary according to whatever tin you're using. They are best eaten on the day of making.

MAKES ABOUT 20

150G UNSALTED BUTTER

175G PLAIN FLOUR, PLUS EXTRA FOR DUSTING

1 TEASPOON BAKING POWDER

1 TABLESPOON POPPY SEEDS, PLUS EXTRA
FOR SCATTERING

3 LARGE EGGS

150G CASTER SUGAR

A PINCH OF SEA SALT FLAKES

FINELY GRATED ZEST OF 1 UNWAXED LEMON

12–15 TEASPOONS LEMON CURD (SEE PAGE 33
FOR HOMEMADE)

For the lemon glaze
JUICE OF ½ LEMON

150G ICING SUGAR, PLUS EXTRA IF NEEDED

Equipment
2 x 12-HOLE MADELEINE TINS

Melt the butter and use a little to grease the inside of the madeleine tins, ensuring that you get it into every groove and corner. Dust with a little flour, tapping out the excess, then pop in the fridge while you prepare the batter.

Sift the flour and baking powder together in a bowl, stir in the poppy seeds and set aside.

In the bowl of a mixer fitted with the whisk attachment (or using a hand-held electric whisk), whisk the eggs, sugar and salt for about 5 minutes (longer if using a hand-held whisk) until thick, pale and doubled in volume. Add the zest and mix to combine.

Using a large metal spoon and a figure-of-eight action, fold in the sifted dry ingredients. Carefully pour the melted butter around the edge of the bowl and fold in. Cover the bowl with clingfilm and chill for 30 minutes while you preheat the oven to 190°C/gas mark 5.

Drop a rounded teaspoon of batter into the middle of each madeleine indentation and gently spread to fill, leaving a little dip in the middle. Spoon a scant teaspoonful of lemon curd into the dip and cover with a little more batter. Bake on the middle shelf of the oven for about 12 minutes until well risen and golden.

Meanwhile, prepare the glaze. Whisk together the lemon juice and icing sugar until smooth. You want the glaze to be thick enough to just coat the back of a spoon, so add more sugar or a drop of water to adjust the consistency if necessary.

Turn out the madeleines onto a wire rack, leave to cool for a couple of minutes and then brush with a little glaze and finish with a light scattering of poppy seeds.

Lemon Curd

Homemade lemon curd is one of the most delicious things you can possibly make, and once you've done so, you'll never buy a jar of ready-made again. It's a ray of sunshine in a jar and, as it uses only a few simple ingredients that you're likely to have in your kitchen, it can be rustled up at a moment's notice. But as with all simple dishes, the secret to its success lies in using the best possible ingredients you can lay your hands on: the lemons need to be fresh, firm and unwaxed; the butter unsalted and preferably organic; and the eggs should come from the happiest chooks you can find – not only will they taste superior but the colour of the yolks is often deeper, resulting in an even more vibrant curd. Once you've discovered the delights of making lemon curd you could try adding passion fruit pulp or lime zest and juice in place of half of the lemon.

MAKES ABOUT 3 JARS

FINELY GRATED ZEST AND JUICE OF
4 UNWAXED LEMONS

2 LARGE ORGANIC EGGS

3 LARGE ORGANIC EGG YOLKS

225G CASTER SUGAR

125G UNSALTED BUTTER, DICED

A PINCH OF SALT

Equipment
3 X 350G JAM JARS

Put the lemon zest and juice into a heatproof glass or ceramic bowl. Add the whole eggs and yolks and whisk to break up the eggs. Add the sugar, butter and salt, and whisk to combine. Set the bowl over a saucepan of simmering water, but don't allow the bottom of the bowl to come into contact with the simmering water, otherwise you'll end up with scrambled egg rather than silky smooth curd. Stir frequently until the butter has melted and the sugar dissolved.

Continue to cook for about 10 minutes, stirring often, until the curd is hot to the touch and has thickened enough to coat the back of the spoon and will hold a wobbly ribbon trail when the spoon is lifted from the bowl.

Remove from the heat and pass the curd through a fine-mesh sieve into a jug or bowl. Pour into sterilised jars (see page 132) and leave until completely cold before screwing on the lids and chilling. It will keep for up to 10 days in the fridge.

The uses for lemon curd are endless – serve with scones and cream, as a filling for little pastry tarts, madeleines (see page 30) and Victoria sponges, piped into doughnuts, layered in a trifle, stirred into yogurt, folded through ice cream, rolled into roulade, as a topper for meringue... or simply spooned from the jar.

Orange Curd

I like to use a mixture of Seville oranges and regular oranges, and perhaps add a couple of clementines or mandarins into the mix when they are in season.

MAKES 1 LARGE JAR

3–4 ORANGES SCRUBBED IN HOT, SOAPY
WATER AND DRIED

2 LARGE ORGANIC EGGS

2 LARGE ORGANIC EGG YOLKS

125G CASTER SUGAR

75G UNSALTED BUTTER, DICED

A PINCH OF SALT

1 TEASPOON LEMON JUICE

Equipment

400G JAM JAR

Finely grate the zest from three of the oranges and place two-thirds in a heatproof glass or ceramic bowl, setting aside the remaining grated zest for later. Squeeze the juice into a measuring jug – you're going to need 200ml, and any left over is the cook's perk and should be poured into a glass and drunk immediately (unless you're using Seville oranges, in which case it's likely to be too bitter).

Add the juice to the zest in the bowl, then continue making the curd following the method overleaf for Lemon Curd. Once the curd has thickened to the required consistency, mix in the lemon juice to lift and balance the flavours. Add the reserved grated zest once the curd has been strained. Continue as before but using one large sterilised jar.

Ruby Grapefruit Curd

Don't be fooled into thinking that ruby grapefruit juice will yield a blushing pink curd – it's the yolks that give curds most of their colour. But if you wanted to perk up the pinkness of the curd, you could add a tiny drop of pink food colouring paste. Although it's mighty fine as it is, you can flavour this tangy curd with many things, such as vanilla seeds, grated fresh ginger, pink or black peppercorns and star anise. Simply add to the juice as it's reducing.

MAKES 1 LARGE JAR

3 RUBY OR PINK GRAPEFRUITS, SCRUBBED IN
HOT, SOAPY WATER AND DRIED

2 LARGE ORGANIC EGGS

2 LARGE ORGANIC EGG YOLKS

125G CASTER SUGAR

75G UNSALTED BUTTER, DICED

A PINCH OF SALT

1 TEASPOON LEMON JUICE

Equipment

400G JAM JAR

Finely grate the zest from two of the grapefruits and place in a heatproof ceramic or glass bowl. Squeeze the juice from all three and pour into a measuring jug – you'll need 300ml, and any left over should be, in my opinion, chilled and mixed into an early evening cocktail, perhaps with a dash of bourbon and lots of ice. Pour the juice into a small saucepan, bring to the boil over a medium heat and reduce by half. Leave to cool for 10 minutes.

Add the cooled juice to the zest in the bowl, then continue making the curd following the instructions overleaf for Lemon Curd. Once the curd has thickened to the required consistency, mix in the lemon juice to lift and balance the flavours. Continue as before but using one large sterilised jar.

Lime Marshmallows with Passion Fruit Sherbet

Homemade marshmallows are really something special - my niece calls them 'dreamy' and has vowed never to eat store bought again! These light sugary puffs have a hit of lime and an added oopmh of passion fruit sherbert to dip into. Freeze-dried passion fruit powder is available in specialist grocers or online.

MAKES ABOUT 30

SUNFLOWER OIL, FOR OILING

2 TABLESPOONS ICING SUGAR

2 TABLESPOONS CORNFLOUR

6 LEAVES OF PLATINUM-GRADE
LEAF GELATINE

2 LARGE EGG WHITES

A PINCH OF SALT

350G CASTER SUGAR

1 TABLESPOON LIQUID GLUCOSE OR
GOLDEN SYRUP

FINELY GRATED ZEST OF 2 UNWAXED LIMES
AND JUICE OF 1

For the passion fruit sherbet

100G CASTER SUGAR

½ TEASPOON CITRIC ACID

¼ TEASPOON BICARBONATE OF SODA

1 TABLESPOON FREEZE-DRIED PASSION
FRUIT POWDER (AVAILABLE ONLINE OR IN
SPECIALIST GROCERS)

Equipment

20CM SQUARE BAKING TIN

SUGAR THERMOMETER

Lightly oil the baking tin, line with clingfilm or baking parchment and lightly oil this as well. Mix the icing sugar and cornflour together in a small bowl or freezer bag and dust the lined tin with an even coating. Tip any excess back into the bag or bowl and reserve.

Soak the gelatine leaves in a bowl of cold water for 10 minutes until soft. Place the egg whites in the bowl of a mixer fitted with a whisk attachment and add the salt and 1 tablespoon of the caster sugar but don't start mixing just yet.

Tip the remaining caster sugar and glucose or golden syrup into a medium saucepan and add 150ml cold water. Place the pan over a medium heat and stir gently to dissolve the sugar. Raise the heat, pop the sugar thermometer into the pan and bring the mixture to the boil. Cook at a steady boil until the syrup reaches 120°C. Remove from the heat.

At this point, speed and concentration are important. Drain the gelatine and blot with a clean tea towel or kitchen paper. Whisk the egg whites until they hold stiff peaks. Add the gelatine to the hot syrup and stir until completely melted. With the motor running on medium speed, add the syrup to the egg whites in a steady stream. Add the lime juice and continue to whisk for about 6 minutes until the mixture is cool, very glossy white and stiff enough to hold a firm ribbon trail when the whisk is lifted from the bowl. Add the lime zest and mix well.

Scoop the marshmallow into the prepared tin and spread level with a palette knife. Leave to set in a cool place for at least 4 hours.

Meanwhile, tip all the sherbet ingredients into the bowl of a food processor and whizz for 1–2 minutes until finely ground.

Tip the reserved icing sugar mixture onto a large baking tray. Turn the marshmallow out of the tin onto the tray, peel off the lining paper and cut the marshmallow into squares using a greased kitchen knife. Serve with a good sprinkling of the sherbet, plus extra for dipping.

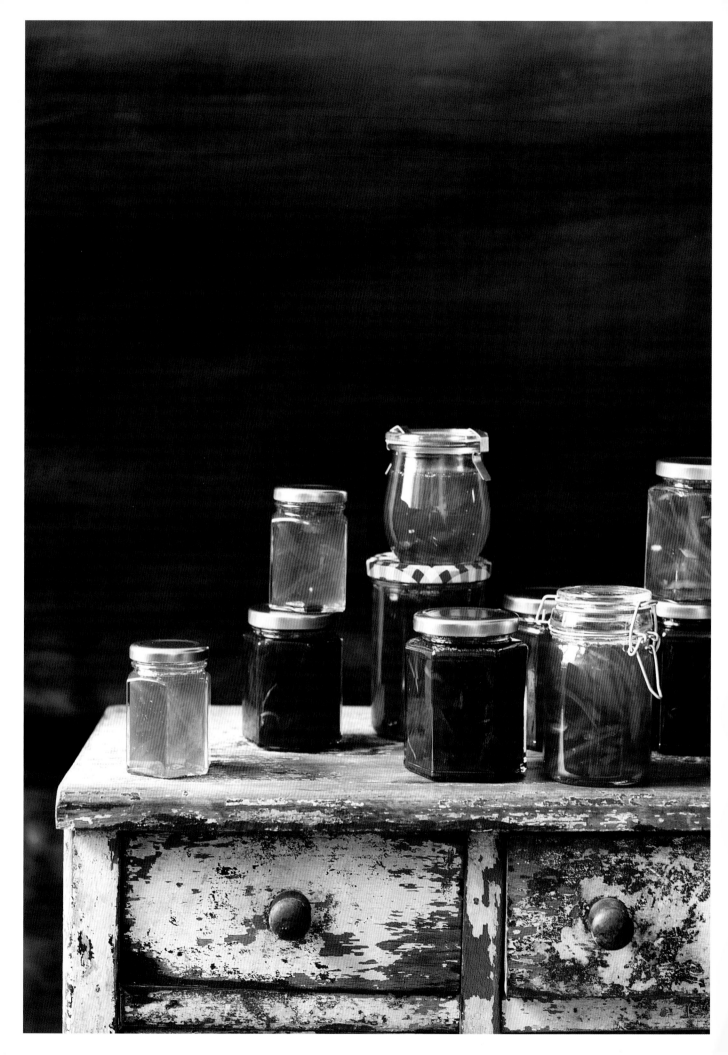

Citrus Marmalade

I'm not going to lie, marmalade making takes time, but it's a small investment to make for the benefit of having a stash of homemade preserves that will last throughout the year and give you great pleasure each morning at your breakfast table. Cutting peel into shreds is somewhat labour intensive, but it's hardly back-breaking stuff and you could either draft in willing helpers or do as I do and stick the radio on and listen to something soothing while rhythmically chopping away. My preference is for a marmalade that is less bitter and with a finer shred, and this really hits the spot. The combination of fruits produces a slightly sweeter, lighter preserve than one made purely from Seville oranges.

MAKES ABOUT 8 JARS

2 SEVILLE ORANGES

3 TANGERINES

1 GRAPEFRUIT

1 UNWAXED LEMON

1.75KG PRESERVING OR GRANULATED SUGAR

Equipment

LARGE STAINLESS STEEL PRESERVING PAN

CLEAN MUSLIN SQUARE AND KITCHEN STRING

8 X 450G JAM JARS

JAM FUNNEL (OPTIONAL)

You will need a combined weight of 950g–1kg fruit. Wash and dry all the fruit, cut in half, squeeze the juice and pour into a large, stainless steel preserving pan. Gather up any pips that have collected in the juicer.

Cut each citrus shell in half again and, using a teaspoon, scrape out the pips and membrane, put with the other pips, tie up tightly in the muslin, then suspend into the preserving pan by tying to the handle.

Using a sharp knife, shred the citrus peel. I like marmalade with finely shredded peels, but if you're of the more chunky persuasion, then please feel free to shred accordingly. Tip all the peels into the pan, along with 1.75 litres of cold water, cover and set aside to soak overnight or for at least 12 hours.

The next day, bring the contents of the pan slowly to the boil over a medium heat. Reduce the heat, half cover the pan and simmer gently for about 1 hour, or until the peels are very soft and can be squashed when pressed between your fingers. This is a very important as, once the sugar is added, the peels will not soften any further.

Preheat the oven to 150°C/gas mark 2. Tip the sugar into a heatproof bowl and warm in the oven for 10 minutes. Pop two saucers into the fridge ready to test for a set. Wash the jam jars and lids in hot, soapy water and dry. Place the jars on a baking tray and heat in the oven to sterilise. Do not heat the lids as they can melt.

Remove the muslin bag and set aside on a plate until cool enough to handle. Squeeze the pectin-filled juice from the muslin bag into the pan and discard the bag.

Add the warmed sugar and stir gently until dissolved. Bring to the boil and continue to cook at a steady rolling boil for about 30 minutes until setting point has been reached. Start testing for set after 15 minutes. Drop a teaspoonful of the preserve onto one of the chilled saucers, leave it for 30 seconds and then push the preserve with the tip of your finger. If it wrinkles, it's ready; if not, cook for a further 5 minutes and test again. Test every 5 minutes until setting point has been reached.

Once the marmalade has reached setting point, remove the pan from the heat, scoop off any scum with a slotted spoon and leave the marmalade to cool for about 10 minutes. If you bottle it without cooling, the peels will rise to the top rather than be evenly distributed.

Pour or ladle into a jug and pour into the warm sterilised jars. Wipe the jars to remove any drips and tightly seal with lids. Leave until completely cold before labelling. Store in a cool, dark cupboard for up to 1 year and up to 3 months in the fridge after opening.

Seville Orange Marmalade with Whisky and Ginger

Your window of opportunity for making real marmalade using Seville oranges is pretty small – the season runs from about late December to early February in Europe, weather and harvest depending, so seize the fruit and the moment! If you happen to have some sticky stem ginger in your cupboards, then finely chop a couple of nuggets and add to the pan with the whisky for an extra ginger hit.

MAKES ABOUT 8 JARS

1KG SEVILLE ORANGES

1 LEMON

5CM PIECE OF FRESH GINGER

2KG PRESERVING OR GRANULATED SUGAR

4 TABLESPOONS WHISKY OR GINGER WINE

Equipment

LARGE STAINLESS STEEL PRESERVING PAN

CLEAN MUSLIN SQUARE AND KITCHEN STRING

8 x 450G JAM JARS

JAM FUNNEL (OPTIONAL)

Before starting give the oranges a good scrub in hot soapy water to remove any dust or wax. Cut each fruit in half and squeeze out all of the juice. Any pips and pith that gather in the juicer should be tipped into a bowl and set aside. Pour the resulting juice, and that from the lemon too, into a large stainless steel preserving pan.

Follow the method given for the Citrus Marmalade on page 39 in steps 2 and 3 to prepare the orange peels, then tip into the preserving pan and cover with 2 litres of cold water. Peel and finely shred the ginger, then add to the preserving pan. Mix well, cover, and set aside for 24 hours.

The next day, again follow the method for cooking the Citrus Marmalade from step 4 onwards. Start testing for a set after 30 minutes, and once it has reached setting point, add the whisky or ginger wine to the pan and boil for a further 30 seconds, then slide the pan off the heat. Leave to cool and then bottle and store as before.

Bergamot Preserve

As this preserve is unusual, I like to bottle it into smaller jars than normal to make a rather special gift.

MAKES 4 SMALL JARS

700G BERGAMOTS (ABOUT 5–6 FRUITS)

2 SWEET ORANGES

1.5KG PRESERVING OR GRANULATED SUGAR

Equipment

STAINLESS STEEL PRESERVING PAN

CLEAN MUSLIN SQUARE AND KITCHEN STRING

4 x 250G JAM JARS

JAM FUNNEL (OPTIONAL)

Scrub the fruit in hot soapy water to remove any wax or dust. Remove the zest from half of the bergamots using a vegetable peeler and cut into fine shreds. Cut all of the fruit in half, squeeze the juice and pour into a preserving pan. Scoop the seeds and any pithy membrane from the juicer and the shells of the squeezed out fruits onto a square of clean muslin. Tie it up tightly, then suspend into the preserving pan by tying to the handle. Add 1.75 litres of cold water, cover and set aside for 24 hours to soften the peels.

The next day, follow the method given for Citrus Marmalade on page 39 from step 4 onwards. Store in a cool, dark cupboard for up to 6 months and in the fridge after opening.

Orange and Beet Salad

For many years my family lived in South West France, and during the summer months we ate nearly every meal outside under a walnut tree in the garden. Lunches often came in the form of salads prepared by my stepfather and were composed from whatever was good that day in his vegetable garden. The salads were arranged as little piles of ingredients on large plates with often up to ten different items, and this is my slightly smaller take on that. Oranges are wonderful when combined with beetroot, bitter salad leaves and wafer-thin slices of salty air-dried ham. Feel free to add as many other elements to this salad as you feel fit or have to hand – thinly sliced fennel, radishes and crisp French beans would all be delicious. The only thing missing is the French sunshine.

SERVES 4–6

6 SMALL BEETROOTS

6 TABLESPOONS EXTRA VIRGIN OLIVE OIL

2 TABLESPOONS SHERRY VINEGAR

1 SMALL GARLIC CLOVE, CRUSHED

4 ORANGES

2 HEADS OF RED CHICORY

2 HEADS OF WHITE CHICORY

BUNCH OF DANDELION (PISENLIT) LEAVES

50G PECANS, ROUGHLY CHOPPED

2 TABLESPOONS SNIPPED CHIVES

12 SLICES OF AIR-DRIED HAM

SALT AND FRESHLY GROUND BLACK PEPPER

Cook the unpeeled beetroots in a medium saucepan of salted boiling water for about 20 minutes, depending on size, until tender when tested with the point of a knife. Drain and peel while still warm. Cut into quarters (or slimmer wedges if on the large side) and tip into a bowl.

In a small bowl, whisk together the olive oil, sherry vinegar, garlic and a good seasoning of salt and black pepper. Drizzle 1–2 tablespoons of the dressing over the warm beetroots and leave until cold.

Cut a thin slice off the top and bottom of each orange so that they sit upright on the chopping board. Using a small, sharp serrated knife and a sawing action, working from the top to the bottom, cut the peel and all the pith away from the fruit in strips all the way round. You should end up with denuded barrel-shaped oranges. Cut each segment away from the orange membrane and into a bowl.

Separate the chicory and dandelion leaves, wash in cold water and dry on a clean tea towel. Divide between serving plates and add a pile of beetroot and orange segments. Scatter over the pecans and chives, and drizzle with the dressing. Drape the slices of air-dried ham alongside, season with salt and black pepper and serve.

Orange-scented Churros with Caramel Orange Chocolate Sauce

What's not to love about churros? Crisp, fried dough strips, tossed in sugar and served while still warm with a rich chocolate dipping sauce… only these ones are better! They have a hint of orange zest and a smattering of grated chocolate in the mix. The orange theme continues in a caramel chocolate fashion for the dipping sauce.

SERVES 4–6

For the churros batter

100G UNSALTED BUTTER, DICED

A GOOD PINCH OF SEA SALT

175G PLAIN FLOUR

¼ TEASPOON BAKING POWDER

3 LARGE EGGS, LIGHTLY BEATEN

1 TEASPOON ORANGE FLOWER WATER

FINELY GRATED ZEST OF 1 ORANGE

1.5 LITRES SUNFLOWER OIL, FOR DEEP-FRYING

40G DARK CHOCOLATE, COARSELY GRATED

200G CASTER SUGAR

For the chocolate sauce

125G CASTER SUGAR

FRESHLY SQUEEZED JUICE OF 2 ORANGES

150ML DOUBLE CREAM

100G DARK CHOCOLATE, FINELY CHOPPED

1 TEASPOON UNSALTED BUTTER

A GOOD PINCH OF SEA SALT FLAKES

Equipment

SUGAR THERMOMETER

LARGE PIPING BAG FITTED WITH A LARGE STAR NOZZLE

Place the butter in a medium saucepan, add 200ml of cold water and the sea salt and set over a low heat until the butter has melted. Meanwhile, sift the flour and baking powder onto a sheet of baking parchment. Bring the water and butter mixture to a rolling boil and then immediately remove from the heat. Working quickly, tip the dry ingredients into the pan and beat vigorously with a wooden spoon until the mixture comes away from the sides of the pan in a smooth, glossy mass. Tip into a bowl and leave to cool for 3–4 minutes.

Gradually add the beaten eggs to the batter, mixing well after each addition, until the mixture is smooth, glossy and drops reluctantly from the spoon. Add the orange flower water and orange zest and mix to combine. Cover the bowl with a clean tea towel and leave to cool to room temperature.

Meanwhile, make the sauce. In a small, heavy-bottomed saucepan, heat the sugar with 1–2 tablespoons of hot water over a low heat without stirring until dissolved. Bring to the boil and cook until the syrup becomes amber-coloured. Take off the heat and add the juice – the caramel will hiss and splutter and may well harden in the pan. Return to a low heat to re-melt it. Once it's silky smooth, add the cream and heat to just below boiling point. Remove from the heat, add the chocolate, butter and sea salt flakes and stir until smooth.

Pour the sunflower oil into a large, wide sauté pan and place over a medium heat. Heat the oil to 180°C. Stir the grated chocolate into the batter, then scoop into the piping bag. Tip the sugar onto a large tray and line another with a double or triple thickness of kitchen paper. Pipe four long fingers of batter directly into the hot oil, cutting off each strip with scissors. Don't crowd the pan, as this will lower the oil temperature, resulting in soggy, oily and heavy churros. Cook for about 45 seconds on each side until golden brown and crisp. Remove with a slotted spoon and drain on the kitchen paper. Roll the warm churros in the sugar and serve immediately with the warm chocolate sauce. Ensure the oil comes back up to temperature before cooking the next batch.

Portuguese Lemon Tarts

My *pastel de nata*, or custard tarts, aren't quite classic, as they are laced with lemon, but hopefully they are simpler to make. The pastry, which is similar to puff, takes a bit of forward planning and needs to be started the day before you plan to bake. Nothing, in my opinion, compares to homemade, but if you're short on time then store-bought all butter puff pastry would make an acceptable substitute. They are best eaten on the day of making.

MAKES 20–24

For the pastry

275G PLAIN FLOUR, PLUS EXTRA FOR DUSTING

A GOOD PINCH OF SEA SALT

175G UNSALTED BUTTER, SOFTENED

For the filling

325ML FULL-FAT MILK

JUICE OF 2 LEMONS

FINELY GRATED ZEST OF 1 UNWAXED LEMON

250G CASTER SUGAR

4 LEVEL TABLESPOONS CORNFLOUR

6 LARGE EGG YOLKS

Equipment

2 x 12-HOLE MUFFIN TINS OR SIMILAR-SIZED INDIVIDUAL PIE TINS

Start by making the pastry. Tip the flour into a mixing bowl, add the salt and 175ml cold water and mix until you have an almost smooth dough. Very lightly dust the work surface with flour, tip out the dough and knead very briefly until smooth. Pat into a square, cover with an upturned bowl and leave to rest for 15 minutes.

Lightly dust the work surface with flour and roll the dough into a neat rectangle three times as long as it is wide (about 45 x 15cm) and with one of the shorter sides nearest to you. Mentally divide the rectangle of dough into thirds – each third a rough square shape – and spread 120g of the butter evenly over the middle third. Fold the bottom third up to cover the butter and the top third down to make a neat square shape. Turn the dough 90 degrees clockwise so that the open flap side is now on the left. Roll into a rectangle again and fold the bottom third up into the middle and the top third down again. Carefully wrap with clingfilm and chill for 1 hour.

Lightly dust the work surface with flour and again roll out the dough into a rectangle (about 45x15cm). Fold and roll the dough as before, then chill again for 1 hour.

Lightly dust the work surface once again and roll out the dough into a neat rectangle about 40 x 50cm. Spread the remaining butter over the surface, being careful not to tear the dough. Starting at the edge closest to you, roll the dough into a tight spiral log, trim the ends and cut the log in half to make handling easier. Wrap each log in clingfilm and chill for about 4 hours or overnight until firm.

Meanwhile, in a saucepan, bring the milk, 150ml cold water and the lemon juice slowly to just below boiling point. In a bowl, whisk the lemon zest with the sugar, cornflour and egg yolks. Pour over half the milk mixture, whisk until smooth, then return to the pan and cook over a low heat, whisking constantly, until it has thickened and no longer tastes of cornflour. Remove from the heat, pour into a clean bowl and cover the surface with clingfilm to prevent a skin forming. Leave to cool, then chill until needed.

Preheat the oven to 200°C/gas mark 6. Lightly dust the work surface with flour and cut the dough logs into 1cm-thick slices. Roll out each one to a thin disc about 11cm across. Press the pastry into the tins so that it comes up the sides. Don't worry about trimming off the edges. Scoop a rounded dessertspoonful of the custard into each case. Bake on the middle shelf of the oven for about 25 minutes until the filling is tinged with brown and the pastry is crisp and golden. Leave in the tins for 5–10 minutes, then transfer to a wire rack until cold.

Slow-cooked Shoulder of Lamb with Oranges

I love food like this – something that is utterly delicious and takes little effort but relies heavily on the quality of the ingredients used. In this case, a good hunk of lamb, marinated with aromatic flavourings and slow-cooked to the point of melting. It benefits from overnight marinating, but is the kind of dish that you can pop in the oven and go for a long walk without worrying about it coming to any harm. There's no need to make gravy either – the onions and oranges produce a delicious pan juice that is perfect served with a pile of crunchy fennel seed potatoes or fluffy herby couscous.

SERVES 4–6

1 HEAPED TEASPOON CUMIN SEEDS

1 HEAPED TEASPOON FENNEL SEEDS

2 SMALL DRIED RED CHILLIES

1 TEASPOON ANCHO CHILLI POWDER OR SMOKED PAPRIKA

3 TABLESPOONS OLIVE OIL

3 TABLESPOONS CLEAR HONEY

2KG LAMB SHOULDER ON THE BONE

4–5 SMALL RED ONIONS, QUARTERED

2 SEVILLE OR BITTER ORANGES, SCRUBBED IN HOT, SOAPY WATER AND DRIED, THEN QUARTERED

2 HEADS OF GARLIC, HALVED HORIZONTALLY

1 CINNAMON STICK

2 TABLESPOONS POMEGRANATE MOLASSES

Spoon the cumin and fennel seeds and dried chillies into a small, dry frying pan and place over a low–medium heat for a minute or so until they start to smell aromatic, shaking the pan so that they toast evenly. Lightly grind the toasted spices using a pestle and mortar – don't reduce them to a powder. Add the chilli powder or smoked paprika, olive oil, honey and a seasoning of sea salt and black pepper.

Using a sharp knife, cut 5–6 slashes into the lamb shoulder, to allow the aromatic flavours to really penetrate the meat. Place the lamb in a large freezer bag (or roasting tin if you find this easier) and rub the spice mixture into the meat. Then add the onions, oranges, garlic and cinnamon stick. Massage everything together so that the meat is really well basted, seal the bag (or cover the meat well if it's in a roasting tin) and chill overnight. The next day, bring the lamb back to room temperature and preheat the oven to 190°C/gas mark 5.

Tip everything into a large roasting tin, making sure the lamb is skin-side uppermost and that there is an even distribution of onions, oranges and garlic around the meat. Cook, uncovered, for 20 minutes, then cover the roasting tin tightly with foil, reduce the heat to 150°C/gas mark 2 and cook for a further 2½ hours until the lamb is tender. Remove the foil and return the heat to 190°C/gas mark 5. Spoon the pomegranate molasses over the meat, baste with the pan juices and cook for another 20 minutes until the lamb is nicely browned and sticky.

Leave the lamb to rest in the tin, covered with foil, for a good 20 minutes before pulling the meat from the bone using forks and serving with the pan juices poured over.

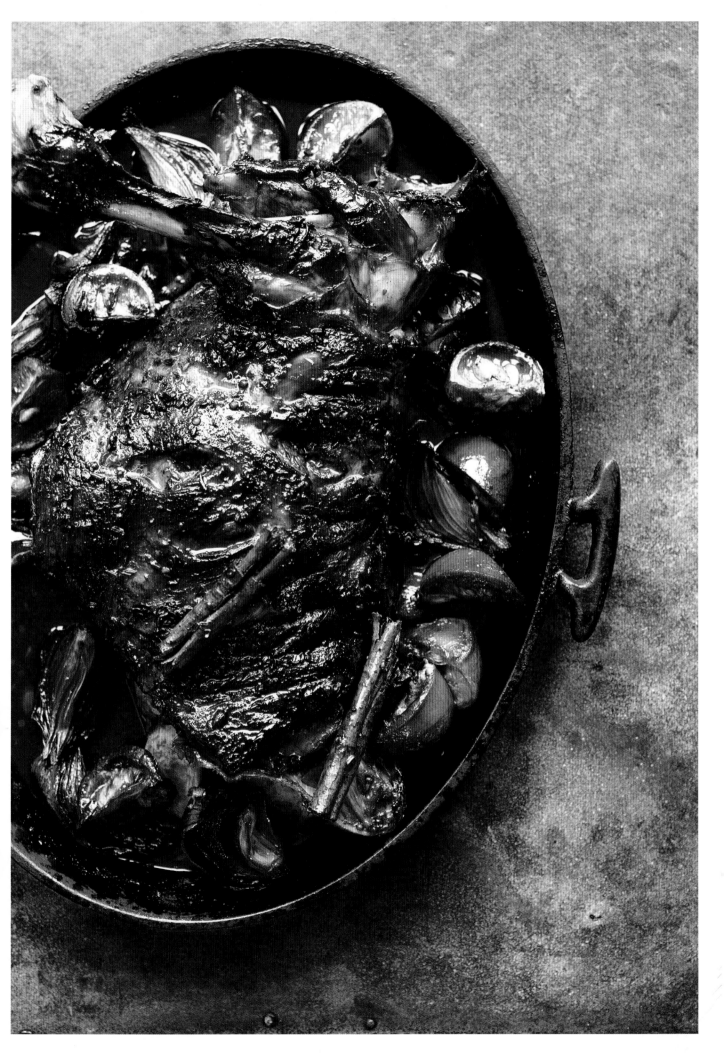

Spring Salad with Lemon Dressing and Goat's Cheese Toasts

I use this lemony dressing for all manner of salads – it goes beautifully with tomatoes and basil, chargrilled courgettes and aubergines, sliced avocados or a simple leaf salad. Gremolata is a classic garnish for osso bucco but it's also another workhorse recipe – scatter it over chargrilled meats, grilled vegetable salads, risotto or grilled fish for an instant lift. Try to buy peas and broad beans still in the pod rather than in ready-prepared packs, or if you are a lucky enough to grow your own, use these – they'll be fresher and more flavoursome.

SERVES 4 AS A STARTER OR LIGHT LUNCH

A LARGE BUNCH OF ASPARAGUS

200G PODDED PEAS

200G PODDED BROAD BEANS

75G BABY LEAF SPINACH

A HANDFUL OF PEA SHOOTS

4 SLICES OF SOURDOUGH BREAD

200G ASH-COVERED YOUNG GOAT'S CHEESE LOG

SALT

For the gremolata

2 GARLIC CLOVES, FINELY CHOPPED

4 TABLESPOONS FINELY CHOPPED FLAT-LEAF PARSLEY

FINE STRIPS OF ZEST FROM AN UNWAXED LEMON

2 TABLESPOONS ROUGHLY CHOPPED PITTED GREEN OLIVES

SEA SALT FLAKES AND FRESHLY GROUND BLACK PEPPER

For the lemon dressing

JUICE OF THE ZESTED LEMON USED FOR THE GREMOLATA

4 TABLESPOONS EXTRA VIRGIN OLIVE OIL, PLUS EXTRA FOR DRIZZLING

1 TEASPOON DIJON MUSTARD

1 TEASPOON CLEAR HONEY, OR TO TASTE

SEA SALT FLAKES AND FRESHLY GROUND BLACK PEPPER

Trim the asparagus by snapping off the woody ends, then cut each spear into 5–6cm lengths. Bring a saucepan of salted water to the boil and blanch the asparagus for 3 minutes or until tender, then refresh in a bowl of iced water. Not only will this stop the asparagus cooking any further but it will preserve the beautiful, vibrant emerald green colour. Blanch the peas in the same pan for 1–2 minutes and add to the asparagus. Cook the broad beans in the same water for 1–2 minutes and then drain through a colander. Rinse the beans under cold water and then slip each one from its outer jacket to reveal the bright green, tender bean inside. Drain all the veggies and pat dry on kitchen paper.

To make the gremolata, combine all the ingredients in a small bowl and season with salt and black pepper.

Next make the dressing. Squeeze the juice from the lemon into a bowl, add the olive oil and mustard and whisk to combine. Taste and add the honey and a seasoning of salt and pepper. Toss the beans, peas and asparagus in the dressing and arrange on plates with the baby leaf spinach and pea shoots.

Toast the sourdough on both sides under the grill. Slice the goat's cheese into 1cm-thick discs and place one slice on each piece of toast. Flash the cheese under the grill again until it starts to soften. Spoon the gremolata alongside, drizzle with a little more oil and serve immediately with the salad.

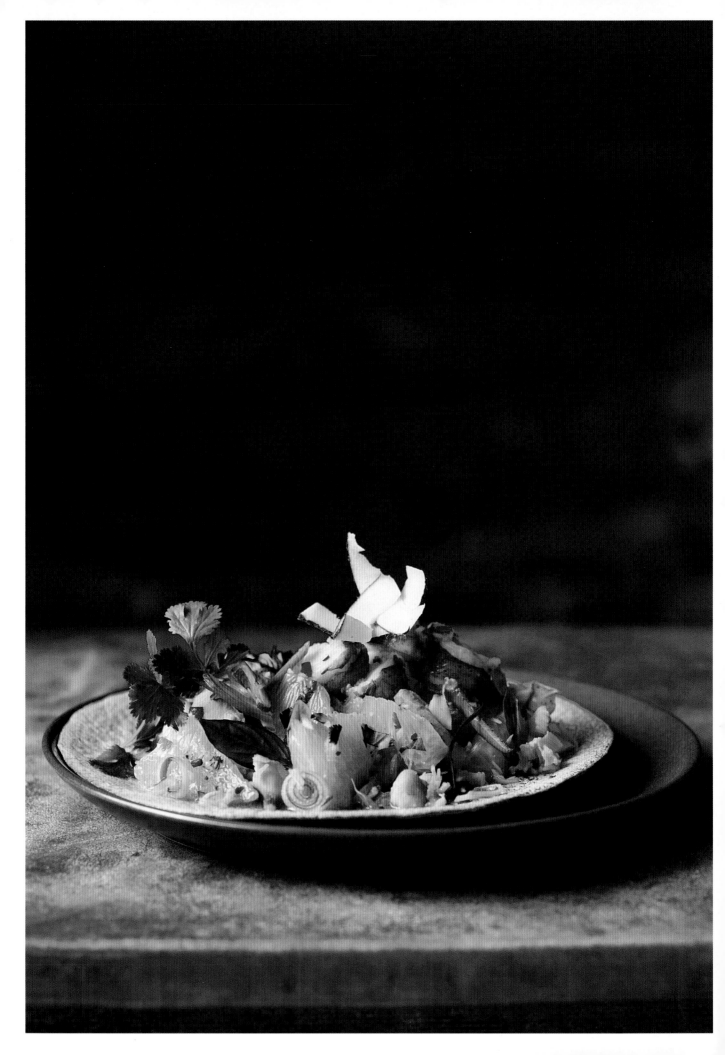

Thai Pomelo Salad with Lobster and Crab

In Thailand, a variation of this salad minus the seafood is often served alongside curries, but in this instance I've added lobster and crab to make it substantial enough to be served as the hero. If lobster is hard to find or blows your budget, try using freshly cooked tiger prawns or chargrilled squid instead.

SERVES 4 AS A LIGHT LUNCH OR PART OF A SHARING TABLE

For the dressing

2–3 BIRD'S EYE CHILLIES, DESEEDED AND FINELY CHOPPED

2 GARLIC CLOVES, FINELY CHOPPED

3 FRESH LIME LEAVES, FINELY SHREDDED

1 LARGE OR 2 SMALL LEMONGRASS STALKS, INNER STALKS TRIMMED AND FINELY SLICED

1 TABLESPOON GRATED FRESH GINGER

4 TABLESPOONS LIME JUICE

3 TABLESPOONS PALM SUGAR OR GOLDEN CASTER SUGAR

3 TABLESPOONS FISH SAUCE

3 TABLESPOONS RICE WINE VINEGAR

For the salad

2 POMELOS

1 COOKED LARGE LOBSTER

200G FRESHLY COOKED WHITE CRABMEAT

A HANDFUL OF CORIANDER LEAVES

A HANDFUL OF THAI BASIL

FLESH OF ¼ FRESH COCONUT, SHAVED INTO STRIPS USING A VEGETABLE PEELER

3 RED SHALLOTS, FINELY SLICED

Start by making the dressing. Pound the chillies, garlic, lime leaves and lemongrass together using a pestle and mortar. Add the remaining dressing ingredients and mix until the sugar has dissolved.

Cut a slice off the top and bottom of the pomelos. Stand the pomelos upright on the chopping board and, using a serrated knife and a sawing motion, slice the skin in strips from top to bottom, removing all the pith as you do so. Neatly cut or tear the pomelo into segments by slicing in between the membranes. Gently toss the segments in three-quarters of the dressing and set aside to soak up the flavours while you deal with the shellfish.

Remove the lobster claws and crack the shells with a rolling pin or meat mallet. Carefully remove all the claw meat. Twist the head from the lobster body and reserve for making stock along with all the shell. Using kitchen scissors, cut through the shell on the underside of the lobster body from one end to the other. Carefully prise the shell apart and remove the lobster tail in one piece. Slice the tail meat into thick slices. Pick through the crabmeat and remove any traces of shell.

Arrange the pomelo on plates and top with the lobster and crabmeat. Scatter with the coriander and basil, and spoon over the remaining dressing. Finish with a flourish of shaved coconut and sliced shallots and serve immediately.

Pomelos are native to South East Asia and can be found in most good Thai or specialist Asian grocers, where you can also pick up most of the other ingredients needed to make this salad. Pomelos have a thick, smooth yellowish-green skin and are nearest in looks to a grapefruit, although they can be at least twice the size and often weigh in at over 1kg, but a large proportion of this is skin and pith.

Tuna Crudo Salad with Pink Grapefruit and Citrus Dressing

Not only does this salad look very pretty, it tastes rather marvellous too. If you prefer, you could use cooked prawns in place of the tuna and wild rocket instead of the mizuna. However, if you have a garden or even a small terrace, it's worth growing a few pots of mizuna, as these peppery, sharp salad leaves are about the easiest thing to grow and really add an extra dimension to the salad bowl.

SERVES 4 AS A LIGHT DISH

1 HEAD OF FENNEL

4 TABLESPOONS RICE VINEGAR

2 TABLESPOONS CASTER SUGAR

A PINCH OF SALT

2 PINK GRAPEFRUITS

250G SUSHI-GRADE FRESH TUNA

A HANDFUL OF MIZUNA

RED SHISO OR OTHER MICRO HERBS OR SPROUTS

1 TABLESPOON SESAME SEEDS, LIGHTLY TOASTED

NANAMI TOGARSHI (JAPANESE CHILLI SEASONING)

For the dressing

2 TABLESPOONS SOY SAUCE

2 TABLESPOONS GRAPEFRUIT, ORANGE OR MANDARIN JUICE

4 TEASPOONS YUZU OR LIME JUICE

4 TABLESPOONS SESAME OIL

FRESHLY GROUND BLACK PEPPER

Start by lightly pickling the fennel. Trim the fennel, cut into quarters and very finely slice (this is best done using a mandolin if you have one), then tip into a glass or ceramic bowl. Combine the rice vinegar and sugar in a small saucepan, add the salt and bring to the boil, swirling the pan to dissolve the sugar. Pour the hot pickling liquid over the fennel and set aside for 30 minutes to soften while you prepare the remaining salad ingredients.

Using a sharp knife, cut a thin slice off the top and bottom of each grapefruit. Sit the grapefruit upright on the chopping board and cut the skin away from the fruit in strips, working from top to bottom, so that you end up with a neat barrel shape with no pith remaining. Neatly cut the grapefruit segments away from the membrane and set aside. Squeeze the juice from the membrane into a bowl – you will need 2 tablespoons for the dressing.

To make the dressing, tip all the ingredients into a small bowl with the grapefruit juice and whisk briefly to combine.

Slice the tuna into neat bite-sized pieces and arrange on plates. Drain the fennel from the pickling liquid and arrange around the tuna with the grapefruit segments. Scatter the mizuna and shiso or other micro herbs or sprouts around, sprinkle with the toasted sesame seeds, drizzle with the dressing and season with nanami togarshi. Serve immediately.

Berries & Soft Fruit

Full of bright sweetness, like a jewel box of colours that marks the start of summer, I don't know anyone who doesn't love a bowl of berries.

The season for berries and soft fruit spans the months from late spring to late summer, starting with almost neon pink forced or indoor rhubarb in early spring and ending with black figs heralding the start of autumn. With a role call of strawberries, raspberries, gooseberries, currants, blueberries and blackberries taking their turn to shine in the high summer months, for the cook this is a time of plenty. Although most berries are now available all year round, those that have been imported from the other side of the world months after your local season has finished will be lacking in flavour, sparkle and sweetness that can only come from fruit picked and eaten in a matter of days.

If you are lucky enough to have your own garden or pick-your-own fruit farm nearby, then you will be aware of how much better soft fruit tastes when picked from the bush at optimum ripeness, still warm from the sunshine and heavy with sweet juice. I remember many afternoons as a child spent at a pick-your-own fruit farm – eating my body weight in juicy strawberries and raspberries and never quite managing to fill a basket, which was the purpose of the exercise.

In my kitchen I prefer to use berries for sweet cooking or preserving rather than in savoury food, so in this chapter you'll find recipes for fruit salads, bakes and puddings where I feel that berries are showcased best. When fruit is this good it only requires simple preparation. I can't think of anything nicer than a bowl of garden-grown strawberries served either with a scoop of vanilla sugar to dip them in and a jug of cold rich cream to pour over the top or with crisp, slightly caramelised brown sugar meringues for crunch and texture.

Figs, however, either fresh or dried, marry well with savoury foods and are perfectly matched with tangy cheese, toasted nuts, salty cured ham and bitter salad leaves. Gooseberries and rhubarb are often paired with rich meats and oily fish such as duck and mackerel, but I like gooseberries best when prepared with something creamy and sweet, such as my recipe for posset on page 71.

Fig, Hazelnut and Fennel Soda Bread

Soda bread is possibly the easiest bread to make. It requires no proving or fiddling around with yeast, but does demand a gentle hand and delicate touch to avoid becoming overworked and tough. It's delicious served with good (Irish) butter or with cheese and chutney, and is best eaten on the day of making. I've used soft dried figs here, but you could just as easily use apricots, raisins or dried cranberries, or walnuts or pecans instead of hazelnuts or almonds.

MAKES 1 LARGE LOAF

100G BLANCHED HAZELNUTS

125G SOFT DRIED FIGS

300G PLAIN FLOUR, PLUS EXTRA FOR DUSTING

150G WHOLEGRAIN SPELT OR RYE FLOUR

1 ROUNDED TEASPOON BICARBONATE OF SODA

1 TEASPOON SEA SALT FLAKES

1 TEASPOON FENNEL SEEDS

½ TEASPOON FRESHLY GROUND
BLACK PEPPER

450ML BUTTERMILK, PLUS 2 TABLESPOONS

2 TEASPOONS CLEAR HONEY

A HANDFUL OF SPELT OR RYE FLAKES

Preheat the oven to 180°C/gas mark 4. Lightly dust a large baking tray with flour or cover with baking parchment.

Lightly toast the nuts on a baking tray in the oven for about 4 minutes or until very pale golden. Very roughly chop and set aside. Snip off the tough stalk end from each fig and roughly chop the fruit.

Sift the two flours and bicarbonate of soda into a large mixing bowl, add the salt, fennel seeds and black pepper and mix well. Add the nuts and figs, mix again, then make a well in the middle of the ingredients.

Combine 450ml buttermilk and honey in a jug, pour into the well and, using a large spoon or spatula, mix until just combined. Then, using your hands, gently knead the dough – just enough to bring it together. Lightly flour the work surface, tip the dough out and knead again, keeping it light, as overworking the dough at this stage will result in a leaden loaf. With minimal handling, shape the dough into a round cake shape and transfer to the prepared baking sheet. Brush the top of the loaf with remaining 2 tablespoons of buttermilk. Using a long, sharp knife, score a deep cross in the top and scatter with the spelt or rye flakes. Bake on the middle shelf of the oven for about 35 minutes or until golden brown and the loaf sounds hollow when tapped on the base. Flip the bread over onto its top and bake for a further 3–4 minutes, then transfer to a wire rack until cold.

Fig Chutney

I'm giving you two options for a fig relish to serve with cheese or cold cuts here. One uses fresh and the other soft dried figs. I like both equally, but as fresh figs aren't always so easy to find, I often resort to using dried. Neither chutney nor relish are the types that you need to store for months on end before opening to allow the vinegar to mellow – they can be eaten pretty much straight away.

Fresh

MAKES 2 JARS

8 LARGE FRESH FIGS

1 ONION OR 2 BANANA SHALLOTS, FINELY CHOPPED

5CM PIECE OF FRESH GINGER, FINELY GRATED

200G SOFT LIGHT BROWN SUGAR

150ML CIDER VINEGAR

2 TEASPOONS YELLOW MUSTARD SEEDS

1 CINNAMON STICK

1 BAY LEAF

A PINCH OF ALLSPICE

SALT AND FRESHLY GROUND BLACK PEPPER

Equipment
2 x 450G JAM JARS

Trim the tough stalk from each fig, roughly chop the fruit and tip into a large, stainless steel saucepan. Add all the remaining ingredients and season well. Place the pan over a low–medium heat and stir frequently until the sugar has dissolved.

Bring to the boil and then, keeping the heat at a gentle simmer, cook for about 30 minutes, stirring frequently to prevent the chutney scorching on the base of the pan, until it has turned into a tender, glossy, sticky relish.

Remove the cinnamon stick and bay leaf, spoon into sterilised jam jars (see page 132) and seal with lids. Leave to cool, label and store in a cool, dark cupboard for up to 6 months. Store in the fridge once opened for up to 1 month.

Dried

MAKES 2 JARS

125G SOFT DRIED FIGS, ROUGHLY CHOPPED

50G RAISINS, SULTANAS OR CHOPPED SOFT DRIED DATES

1 LARGE SHALLOT, SLICED

1 SMALL EATING APPLE, PEELED AND DICED

100G LIGHT MUSCOVADO SUGAR

125ML CIDER VINEGAR

1 TEASPOON FINELY GRATED ORANGE ZEST

1 CINNAMON STICK

1 BAY LEAF

SALT AND FRESHLY GROUND BLACK PEPPER

Equipment
2 x 450G JAM JARS

Tip the figs into a large, stainless steel saucepan. Add the raisins, sultanas or chopped dates – whichever you prefer – along with all the remaining ingredients, except the seasoning. Place the pan over a low–medium heat and stir frequently until the sugar has dissolved.

Bring to the boil, then reduce to a simmer and cook for about 25 minutes, stirring frequently, until thickened, glossy and jammy.

Remove the cinnamon stick and bay leaf, season with salt and black pepper and leave to cool, then spoon into sterilised jam jars (see page 132) and seal with lids. Store in the fridge for 2 months.

Fig and Goat's Cheese Tart

This little tart is just perfect to serve for a light lunch – not only does it looks pretty but it takes no time at all to prepare and is super tasty to boot. All it needs is a salad of some peppery leaves such as wild rocket and mizuna, a drizzle of balsamic vinegar dressing and a light scattering of Parmesan shavings.

SERVES 4

PLAIN FLOUR, FOR DUSTING

250G ALL-BUTTER PUFF PASTRY

2 MEDIUM EGGS

1 MEDIUM EGG YOLK

150ML DOUBLE CREAM

4–6 FRESH FIGS

100G GORGONZOLA OR SOFT GOAT'S CHEESE

2 TABLESPOONS PINE NUTS

2 SPRIGS OF THYME, LEAVES PICKED

SALT AND FRESHLY GROUND BLACK PEPPER

AGED BALSAMIC VINEGAR AND EXTRA VIRGIN OLIVE OIL, FOR DRIZZLING

Equipment

35 x 11CM TART TIN

Lightly dust the work surface with flour and roll the pastry out into a rectangle 3cm bigger than the tart tin on all sides. Carefully lift the pastry into the tin – being careful not to stretch the pastry – and press it into the corners, lining the base and sides evenly. Pop into the freezer for 30 minutes while you preheat the oven to 200°C/gas mark 6 and place a solid baking tray on the middle shelf to heat up.

Prepare the filling. In a bowl, beat the whole eggs and egg yolk with the cream until thoroughly combined and season well with salt and black pepper. Trim the tough stalk from each fig and cut each fig in half. Prick the base of the pastry case with a fork and pour in the egg mixture. Crumble the cheese on top and arrange the fig halves evenly between the cheese, cut-side uppermost. Scatter with the pine nuts and thyme leaves.

Carefully slide the tart onto the hot baking tray and bake for 15 minutes until the filling has started to set and the pastry starts to turn crisp and golden. Reduce the heat to 180°C/gas mark 4 and cook for a further 15 minutes.

Remove from the oven and leave to cool slightly before serving drizzled with aged balsamic vinegar and extra virgin olive oil.

Fig and Blue Cheese Salad

This is barely a recipe – more of a serving suggestion, but a mighty fine one at that. A stroll around a French or Italian market in early autumn will provide all the ingredients necessary for this salad. Perfectly ripe figs, tangy, grassy blue cheese such as a goat's milk Persillé du Marais, Cote Hill Blue, Roquefort, Gorgonzola or Regalis and slices of Ibérico, Bayonne, Serrano or Parma ham. Packaged in waxed paper and eaten while admiring the view in a picturesque spot somewhere… the best things are often the simplest.

SERVES 3–4

2 HEADS OF CHICORY

1 HEAD OF RADICCHIO OR TREVISO TARDIVE

200G BLUE CHEESE (SEE RECIPE INTRODUCTION)

A GOOD HANDFUL OF CHOPPED TOASTED HAZELNUTS

6 RIPE FIGS

8 SLICES OF CURED HAM (SEE RECIPE INTRODUCTION)

A GENEROUS GLUG OF FRUITY EXTRA VIRGIN OLIVE OIL

A NOT-SO-GENEROUS GLUG OF AGED BALSAMIC VINEGAR

SALT AND FRESHLY GROUND BLACK PEPPER

SOURDOUGH BREAD, TO SERVE

Wash the salad leaves in cold water and dry on a clean tea towel, then arrange on a plate. Crumble over the cheese and scatter over the hazelnuts. Cut or tear the figs into quarters or bite-sized pieces and arrange over the leaves with the slices of ham.

Drizzle over the olive oil and balsamic vinegar, season with salt and black pepper and serve with some crusty sourdough bread to mop up the dressing.

Gooseberry Jelly

If making this at the start of the gooseberry season when elderflowers are still in bloom, pick a handful of blowsy flower heads and add to the fruit as it cooks to add a fragrant, floral note. As always when using fresh flowers in cooking, ensure that they are washed, not picked from the roadside, bug free and unsprayed with chemicals. Add a dash of elderflower cordial if you prefer, but go easy, as you don't want to overpower the delicate gooseberry flavour.

Leaf gelatine has a milder flavour than powdered and is available in different setting strengths – I always use platinum grade, which gives a stronger set for fewer leaves, and is available in most supermarkets. I have given two quantities here: use the lesser one if you plan to serve the jelly in pretty glasses with a slightly softer set and the higher quantity for a firmer, wobbly jelly set into a mould and turned out on a plate. If planning on the latter, I'd recommend that you make the jelly at least 24 and up to 48 hours before serving – it will hold its shape better the longer you leave it to set.

MAKES 1 LARGE JELLY OR 6–8 GLASSES

1.25KG GOOSEBERRIES, RINSED (NO NEED TO TOP AND TAIL)

125–150G CASTER SUGAR, TO TASTE

7–9 LEAVES OF PLATINUM-GRADE LEAF GELATINE (SEE RECIPE INTRODUCTION)

SUNFLOWER OIL, FOR OILING (IF USING A MOULD)

WHITE CURRANTS OR ELDERFLOWERS, TO DECORATE

JERSEY POURING CREAM, TO SERVE

Equipment
JELLY BAG
1 LITRE JELLY MOULD (OPTIONAL)

If you are partial to the odd cocktail, do as I do and, once you've strained off all the gooseberry juice, tip the fruit pulp into a preserving jar, add a handful of elderflowers and pour in a bottle of gin. Seal tightly, give the jar a shake and leave in the fridge for 1 month, shaking every other day or when you remember. Strain through muslin and use as you see fit – it's good as a Martini and gives a G&T an unusual twist.

Tip the gooseberries into a large saucepan with 500ml cold water. Set over a low–medium heat, half cover and bring slowly to the boil. Reduce the heat to a gentle simmer and cook until the berries have burst, stirring with a wooden spoon to break up the fruit.

Pour into a jelly bag suspended over a large bowl. Allow the juice to slowly drip into the bowl but do not squeeze the bag or prod the fruit – leave the juice to drip through until the skin and seeds are all that's left in the bag, which can take a good few hours. Measure the resulting juice – you should have about 1 litre – add the sugar to taste and stir well to dissolve.

Soak the gelatine leaves in a large bowl of cold water for 10 minutes to soften. Pour half the gooseberry juice into a pan, heat to just boiling and then remove from the heat. Drain the gelatine leaves, squeeze out any excess water and blot quickly on a clean tea towel or kitchen paper, then add to the hot juice. Stir well until completely melted, add the reserved juice, stirring to combine, and leave to cool to room temperature. Pour into glasses or a very lightly oiled jelly mould, then place on a tray, slide into the fridge and leave until set. This will take at least 24 hours for glasses and longer - see introduction - for moulds.

Quickly dip the jelly mould, if using, in a bowl of just-boiled water to loosen the sides and carefully turn out onto a serving plate. Serve the jelly or jellies decorated with white currants or elderflowers, with a jug of cold Jersey pouring cream.

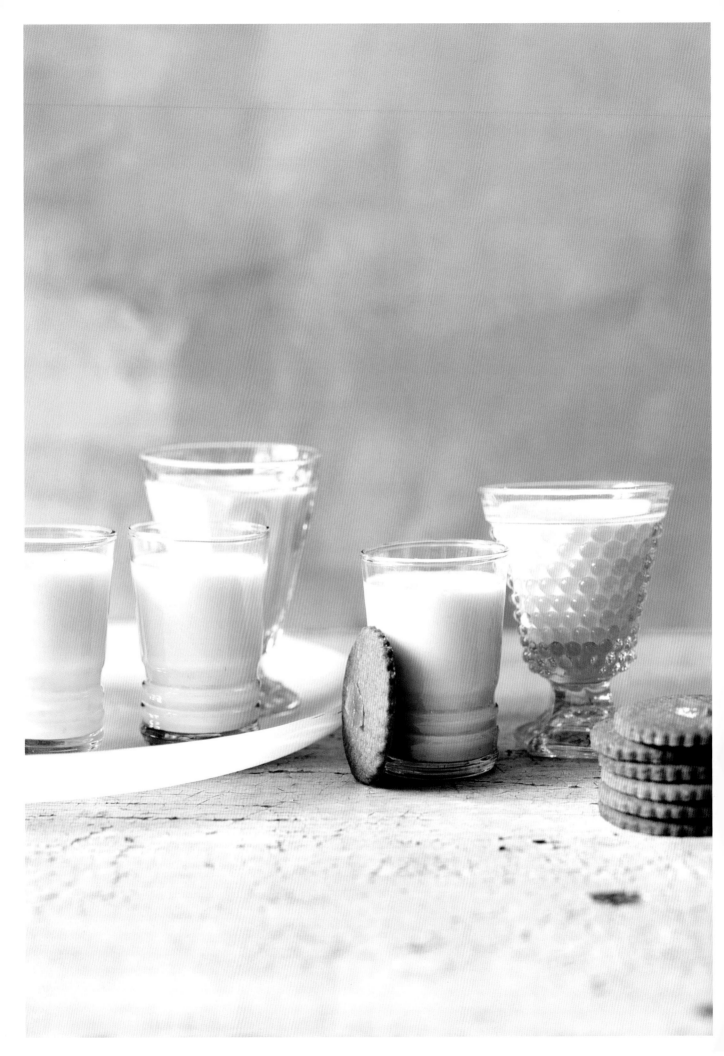

Gooseberry Posset with Gingery Thins

Most people are more familiar with posset made from lemons. In this twist I've stuck with the usual three ingredients but used cooked gooseberries in place of the lemons, which are often folded into whipped cream to make a fool – something I love for its simplicity and the fact that it's somewhat old-fashioned. The result is an altogether more sophisticated dessert, though no harder to make. As posset is quite rich, I like to serve it in small, elegant glasses with something crisp and snappy on the side, so while the posset is chilling, use your time wisely and rustle up these Gingery Thins.

SERVES 4–6; MAKES ABOUT 30 BISCUITS

For the posset

400G GOOSEBERRIES, RINSED, TOPPED
AND TAILED

125G CASTER SUGAR

450ML DOUBLE CREAM

For the gingery thins

125G UNSALTED BUTTER, SOFTENED

50G LIGHT MUSCOVADO SUGAR

1 TABLESPOON GOLDEN SYRUP

150G PLAIN FLOUR, PLUS EXTRA FOR DUSTING

25G GROUND ALMONDS

¼ TEASPOON BAKING POWDER

¼ TEASPOON BICARBONATE OF SODA

1 TEASPOON GROUND GINGER

½ TEASPOON GROUND CINNAMON

A GRATING OF NUTMEG

A PINCH OF SALT

3–4 NUGGETS OF STEM OR CANDIED GINGER
(OPTIONAL)

Equipment

FINE-MESH NYLON SIEVE

6CM FLUTED COOKIE CUTTER

Start by making the posset. Tip the gooseberries into a saucepan, add 2 tablespoons of cold water and cover and cook over a low–medium heat for about 15 minutes until the fruit has become really soft and juicy. Pour into a fine-mesh nylon sieve set over a bowl and leave the juice to drip through for about 40 minutes.

Measure the juice – you should have around 175ml – and pour back into the clean pan. Bring to the boil and reduce over a medium heat until you have 100ml remaining. Remove from the heat, add the sugar and stir until dissolved.

Pour the cream into a separate clean saucepan and bring to the boil. Immediately remove the pan from the heat, pour the cream over the gooseberry syrup and whisk until silky smooth. Pour the posset into delicate glasses and leave until cold before covering with clingfilm and popping in the fridge for about 4 hours to set.

Meanwhile, make the biscuits. Cream the butter and sugar in a bowl until pale and fluffy. Mix in the golden syrup. Sift in the dry ingredients and, using a rubber spatula or wooden spoon, mix until the dough comes together into a smooth ball. Flatten into a disc, cover with clingfilm and chill for about 1 hour until firm.

Preheat the oven to 180°C/gas mark 4. Lightly dust the work surface with flour and roll out the dough to a thickness of 2–3mm. Using a 6cm cutter, stamp out rounds and arrange on baking parchment-lined baking trays. Re-roll the scraps and stamp out more biscuits. Thinly slice the stem ginger and place one slice on top of each biscuit.

Bake one tray at a time on the middle shelf of the oven for 9–10 minutes until the biscuits are crisp. Cool slightly on the trays and then transfer to a wire rack until cold.

Gooseberry Meringue Tarts

This nutty tart crust doesn't require overly delicate handling or messing around with a rolling pin, and is therefore ideal for pastry phobes. Gooseberry curd also makes a wonderful filling for a simple Victoria sponge or roulade.

MAKES 8–12

For the pastry

100G BLANCHED HAZELNUTS, TOASTED

125G UNSALTED BUTTER, CHILLED AND DICED

175G PLAIN FLOUR

40G ICING SUGAR

A PINCH OF SALT

1 LARGE EGG YOLK (KEEP THE WHITE FOR THE MERINGUE)

For the gooseberry curd

500G GOOSEBERRIES, WASHED

125G CASTER SUGAR, OR TO TASTE

50G UNSALTED BUTTER, DICED

2 LARGE EGGS

1 LARGE EGG YOLK (KEEP THE WHITE FOR THE MERINGUE)

For the meringue

2 LARGE EGG WHITES – USE ONE FROM THE PASTRY AND ONE FROM THE CURD

A PINCH OF SALT

100G CASTER SUGAR

Equipment

8–12 INDIVIDUAL TART TINS

FINE-MESH NYLON SIEVE

LARGE PIPING BAG FITTED WITH A LARGE STAR NOZZLE

Start by making the pastry. Whizz the hazelnuts in a food processor until finely chopped. Add the butter, flour, icing sugar and salt and pulse until the mixture resembles breadcrumbs. Add the egg yolk, whizz briefly – just enough to bring the dough together – then turn out onto the work surface and gather it together with your hands, although try not to knead it. Shape into a ball, cover with clingfilm and chill for 30 minutes.

Break off a walnut-sized nugget of dough and press it into one of the tart tins, covering the base and sides evenly and pinching off any excess from the top. Repeat with the remaining tins. Prick the bases with a fork and chill for 20 minutes while you preheat the oven to 180°C/gas mark 4.

Bake the tart cases on a baking tray on the middle shelf for about 12–15 minutes until golden and crisp. Leave to cool in the tins. Reduce the oven temperature to 170°C/gas mark 3.

Meanwhile, make the curd. Tip the gooseberries into a pan with 2 tablespoons of cold water, cover and cook over a low–medium heat, stirring occasionally, for about 15 minutes, until very mushy. Push through a fine-mesh nylon sieve into a clean saucepan and cook over a low heat until the purée thickens to a soft jam consistency. Add the sugar and butter and stir until the butter has melted and the sugar dissolved. Whisk together the whole eggs and yolk and add to the pan, stirring constantly. Cook until the mixture thickens enough to coat the back of a spoon, being careful not to allow it to boil. Taste and add more sugar if necessary. Strain into a clean bowl, cover the surface with clingfilm to prevent a skin forming and leave to cool. Spoon the cold curd into the tart cases, filling them to within 2mm of the top and spreading evenly with the back of the spoon.

To make the meringue, tip the egg whites into a large, spotlessly clean mixing bowl, add the salt, then whisk until the egg whites will hold a stiff peak. Gradually add the sugar, a tablespoon at a time, whisking well after each addition, until the meringue is very stiff and glossy.

Scoop into the piping bag and pipe generous swirls on top of the gooseberry curd. Bake for 10 minutes until the meringue is tinged golden brown at the edges. Serve at room temperature.

Rhubarb and Almond Tart

I love this tart with its contrast of sharp yet sweet vanilla and rose-scented rhubarb, nutty frangipane and flaky, buttery pastry. As a bonus, you don't need any fancy tins and it can be knocked up in no time at all. The rhubarb is very lightly softened in syrup before being baked on top of the tart. If you aren't keen on rosewater, simply leave it out, and the frangipane would work equally well with a mixture of half almonds and half pistachios. Whichever way you bake this tart, be sure to serve it with plenty of cold crème fraîche or clotted cream, or with a big scoop of vanilla ice cream.

SERVES 6

400G SLIM-STEMMED FORCED RHUBARB

200G CASTER SUGAR

1–2 TEASPOONS ROSEWATER

½ VANILLA POD, SPLIT IN HALF LENGTHWAYS, OR 1 TEASPOON VANILLA BEAN PASTE

PLAIN FLOUR, FOR DUSTING

375G STORE-BOUGHT ALL-BUTTER PUFF PASTRY

2 TABLESPOONS MILK

1 MEDIUM EGG YOLK, LIGHTLY BEATEN

1 ROUNDED TABLESPOON FLAKED ALMONDS

For the frangipane

75G GROUND ALMONDS

50G UNSALTED BUTTER, SOFTENED

50G CASTER SUGAR

1 MEDIUM EGG

1 TEASPOON VANILLA EXTRACT

1 TEASPOON FINELY GRATED LEMON ZEST

A PINCH OF SALT

Rinse the rhubarb under cold running water and trim the ends. Cut each stem into lengths of about 5cm. Tip the sugar, rosewater and vanilla into a sauté pan and add 200ml cold water. Bring slowly to the boil to dissolve the sugar and then remove from the heat. Add the rhubarb, cover and leave to soften in the hot syrup.

Lightly dust the work surface with flour and roll out the pastry into a rough oval or round shape – I don't think you need worry too much about neatness for this tart so long as the pastry is about 2–3mm thick and the shape about 35 x 25cm. Use a large knife to trim and neaten the edges. Carefully slide the pastry onto a large parchment-lined baking tray, brush the milk around the edge of the pastry and crimp and fold over to create a border. Chill in the fridge for 20 minutes.

Meanwhile, preheat the oven to 200°C/gas mark 6 and make the frangipane. Tip all the ingredients into a mixing bowl and beat well until smooth.

Spread the frangipane over the pastry, leaving a 1–2cm border all the way round as it will spread slightly during cooking. Drain the cooled rhubarb from the syrup and scatter all over the frangipane. Brush the edges of the pastry with the beaten egg yolk and scatter the tart with the flaked almonds. Bake on the middle shelf of the oven for 10 minutes and then reduce the temperature to 180°C/gas mark 4 and cook for a further 20–25 minutes until the frangipane is golden, the pastry crisp and the rhubarb tender. Best served warm, with a light dusting of icing sugar, on the day of making.

Rhubarb and Raspberry Cordial

Homemade cordials are way more delicious and vastly superior to store-bought versions, which can be loaded with preservatives and colours and often barely relate to the fruit from which they are supposedly derived. They're an ideal way to make the most of the season's best produce or to use up a glut. Their shelf life is not long, but if you have space, try freezing the undiluted cordial in ice cube trays and when ready to use dilute with still or sparkling water to taste. I've kept the base recipe simple, but you can add a couple of slices of fresh ginger to the fruit as it cooks, or rose petals – fresh (unsprayed) or dried – vanilla, sliced strawberries or even fresh herbs such as mint or basil.

MAKES ABOUT 750ML

1KG TRIMMED PINK OR SCARLET FORCED RHUBARB, WASHED AND CUT INTO 3–4CM LENGTHS

200G RASPBERRIES

250G CASTER SUGAR

JUICE OF ½ LEMON

100G RASPBERRIES

SODA WATER OR LEMONADE, FOR DILUTING

ICE, TO SERVE

Equipment

JELLY BAG OR LARGE PIECE OF CLEAN MUSLIN

740ML JAR OR BOTTLE

Place the rhubarb in a large saucepan with the raspberries. Add 500ml cold water and bring to a gentle simmer. Half cover the pan and cook the fruit very gently for about 25 minutes until it is very tender and has released lots of lovely pink juice. Remove from the heat and leave to cool for about 2 hours – after which time the juice will have increased in colour quite significantly.

Pour the contents of the pan through a jelly bag (or large piece of clean muslin draped over a fine-mesh sieve) into a clean saucepan – don't be tempted to push and press the pulp, otherwise you'll end up with purée rather than a sparkling clear, bright pink juice. It can take at least an hour for all the juice to strain through, so be patient.

Add the sugar and half the lemon juice and bring slowly to the boil to dissolve the sugar, then simmer gently for 5 minutes. Remove from the heat and leave to cool, then taste and add a dash more lemon juice if needed. Pour into a sterilised jar or bottle (see page 132) and keep refrigerated until ready to use.

Serve over ice diluted with soda water or lemonade, or as a dashing pink gin fizz cocktail – see the recipe below.

Gin and Rhubarb Fizz

SERVES 1

2 PARTS GIN

3 PARTS RHUBARB AND RASPBERRY CORDIAL

DASH OF LEMON JUICE

1 TEASPOON LIGHTLY BEATEN EGG WHITE

ICE CUBES AND TONIC WATER, TO SERVE

RASPBERRIES, TO DECORATE

Place the gin and cordial with the lemon juice and egg white in a cocktail shaker and shake really well.

Half fill a tall glass with ice cubes and tonic water and pour over the pink gin mixture. Decorate with raspberries and perhaps a mint sprig if you're feeling extra fancy.

Strawberry and Rhubarb Compote with Brown Sugar Meringues

Strawberries and rhubarb are a winning combination, one fruit balancing the other for sweet and sour, and the colour of the two fruits together is eye popping. This might seem like a curious way to make meringues, but I find it foolproof. They remain in beautiful peaky mounds rather than spreading during cooking and have crisp, shiny shells and marshmallow centres. Using brown sugar adds a toffee-like note.

SERVES 8

4 TABLESPOONS CASTER SUGAR

3 STRIPS OF ORANGE PEEL

½ VANILLA POD, SPLIT IN HALF LENGTHWAYS

500G SLIM-STEMMED FORCED RHUBARB, WASHED, TRIMMED AND CUT INTO 3–4CM LENGTHS

500G STRAWBERRIES, HULLED AND HALVED OR QUARTERED

300ML DOUBLE CREAM

For the meringues

150G CASTER SUGAR

150G EGG WHITES (3–4 LARGE)

A PINCH OF SALT

1 TEASPOON VANILLA BEAN PASTE

100G LIGHT MUSCOVADO SUGAR

50G WHOLE BLANCHED HAZELNUTS, ROUGHLY CHOPPED

To make the meringues, preheat the oven to 190°C/gas mark 5. Heat the caster sugar in a roasting tin on the middle shelf for 5 minutes until hot to the touch. Meanwhile, tip the egg whites into the bowl of a free-standing mixer fitted with the whisk attachment and add the salt. Once the sugar is hot, turn the oven down to 110°C/gas mark ¼ and whisk the egg whites until they will almost hold a stiff peak.

Quickly tip the hot sugar into the egg whites in one go, add the vanilla and whisk on a fast speed for 3 minutes until the meringue has become stiff and glossy and the sugar has dissolved. Gradually add the muscovado sugar, a tablespoon at a time, whisking constantly until it has been thoroughly incorporated and the meringue has cooled. It should be silky smooth without any grains of sugar. If the sugar hasn't completely dissolved, whisk for another minute or so.

Using a large spoon and palette knife, shape the meringue into 8 mounds on a large baking parchment-lined baking tray. Scatter over the hazelnuts. Bake on the middle shelf of the oven for 1 ¼ hours until crisp. Turn the oven off and leave the meringues inside to cool down for a further 45 minutes.

For the compote, place the sugar, orange peel and vanilla pod in a sauté pan and add 125ml water. Bring slowly to the boil to dissolve the sugar, then add the rhubarb, cover and leave over a gentle heat for 2–3 minutes to soften. Test the rhubarb for doneness with the point of a sharp knife – you want it to be tender but still to hold its shape. If it's still a little firm, cook for a further minute or so. Remove from the heat, add the strawberries and stir in gently. Leave to cool.

Whip the cream until it holds soft luscious peaks – I always do this by hand rather than using an electric whisk, as it reduces the risk of over-whipping. Place one meringue on each plate and pile with a good dollop of whipped cream, then top with a generous spoonful of the compote and a good drizzle of syrup. Eat immediately.

Roasted Strawberry Ice Cream

I've said it many times, but the success of all fruit recipes lies in using ripe, seasonal produce. And this is most certainly the case with strawberries. The best strawberries I have ever eaten come from a small family-run farm in Warwickshire. The berries are sold direct from the farm shop and their season lasts only a couple of weeks – blink and you'll miss them. It would be almost criminal to do anything to them other than to pull out the stalks and eat them au naturel, straight from the punnet.

I'm not normally a fan of cooking with strawberries (unless in jam making), so I'm bending my own rules in this recipe. But roasting the strawberries here really intensifies the flavour, slightly caramelising the sugar and giving a jamminess to the fruit and a boost to the ice cream. If you're not able to make it to a certain farm in Warwickshire, this is an ideal way to use up less-than-perfect fruit.

SERVES 6

1KG STRAWBERRIES, HULLED

175G CASTER SUGAR

1 VANILLA POD, SPLIT IN HALF LENGTHWAYS

2 STRIPS OF PEEL FROM AN UNWAXED LEMON

400ML DOUBLE CREAM

100ML FULL-FAT MILK

4 MEDIUM EGG YOLKS

Equipment

FINE-MESH NYLON SIEVE

ICE-CREAM MAKER

PLASTIC FREEZER BOX

Preheat the oven to 180°C/gas mark 4. Tip the strawberries into an ovenproof ceramic dish or a baking tin lined with baking parchment. Toss with 50g of the sugar and tuck one half of the vanilla pod and the lemon peels amongst the berries. Cook on the middle shelf of the oven for about 40 minutes until slumped and juicy. Discard the vanilla pod half and the peel, and tip the strawberries and all of their juice into the bowl of a food processor and whizz until smooth.

Heat the cream and milk with the remaining vanilla pod half in a saucepan over a medium heat until just below boiling point. Meanwhile, using a hand-held electric whisk, whisk together the remaining 125g of sugar and the egg yolks in a bowl until very pale and thick. Add the hot cream mixture in a steady stream, whisking constantly until smooth. Return to the pan and cook over a low heat, stirring constantly with a wooden spoon, until it thickens enough to coat the back of the spoon, but don't allow it to boil, otherwise the eggs may scramble. Strain through a fine-mesh nylon sieve into a clean bowl and leave to cool completely, then thoroughly chill in the fridge for at least 2 hours but preferably overnight.

Whisk three-quarters of the strawberry purée into the custard and churn in an ice-cream maker according to the manufacturer's instructions. Scoop the ice cream into a plastic freezer box and very lightly stir through the remaining strawberry purée – it should still be visible in ripples. Cover and freeze until firm.

Sunken Chocolate and Raspberry Cake

This cake is more suited as a dessert rather than a tea-time cake. It is almost a baked mousse and it will crack and sink as it cools – which is part of it's charm – beauty in imperfection if you like. Serve with a generous dusting of icing sugar, a mound of fresh raspberries and some cold cream.

SERVES 8–10

250G DARK CHOCOLATE, 70% COCOA SOLIDS, BROKEN INTO PIECES

250G UNSALTED BUTTER, CUT INTO PIECES, PLUS EXTRA FOR GREASING

6 LARGE EGGS, SEPARATED

1 TEASPOON VANILLA EXTRACT

175G CASTER SUGAR

75G SOFT LIGHT BROWN SUGAR

A PINCH OF SALT

75G GROUND ALMONDS

50G PLAIN FLOUR, PLUS EXTRA FOR DUSTING

150G RASPBERRIES, PLUS EXTRA TO SERVE

ICING SUGAR, FOR DUSTING

Equipment

23CM SPRINGFORM CAKE TIN

Preheat the oven to 170°C/gas mark 3. Grease and line the base of the cake tin with greased baking parchment. Lightly dust the tin with flour, tapping out the excess.

Melt the chocolate with the butter in a heatproof bowl, either in the microwave on a low setting or over a saucepan of barely simmering water. Stir until smooth and leave to cool slightly.

Using a free-standing mixer fitted with the whisk attachment, whisk the egg yolks, vanilla extract and caster and brown sugars together until thick and pale, doubled in volume and the mixture leaves a ribbon trail when the whisk is lifted from the bowl, scraping down the sides of the bowl once or twice.

In a separate bowl, whisk the egg whites with the salt until they hold stiff but not dry peaks. Using a large metal spoon, fold the melted chocolate and butter into the egg yolk mixture. Sift the ground almonds and flour into the bowl and fold in along with the raspberries. Fold one-third of the egg whites into the mixture to loosen it and then fold in the remainder, being careful not to knock out the air.

Spoon the mixture into the prepared tin and bake on the middle shelf of the oven for 25–30 minutes until the cake is starting to crack around the edges and the middle is set. Remove from the oven and leave the cake to cool in the tin – it will sink and crack as it cools.

Carefully run a palette knife around the edge of the tin to loosen the cake, remove from the tin and place on a serving plate. Scatter with extra raspberries and dust with icing sugar to serve.

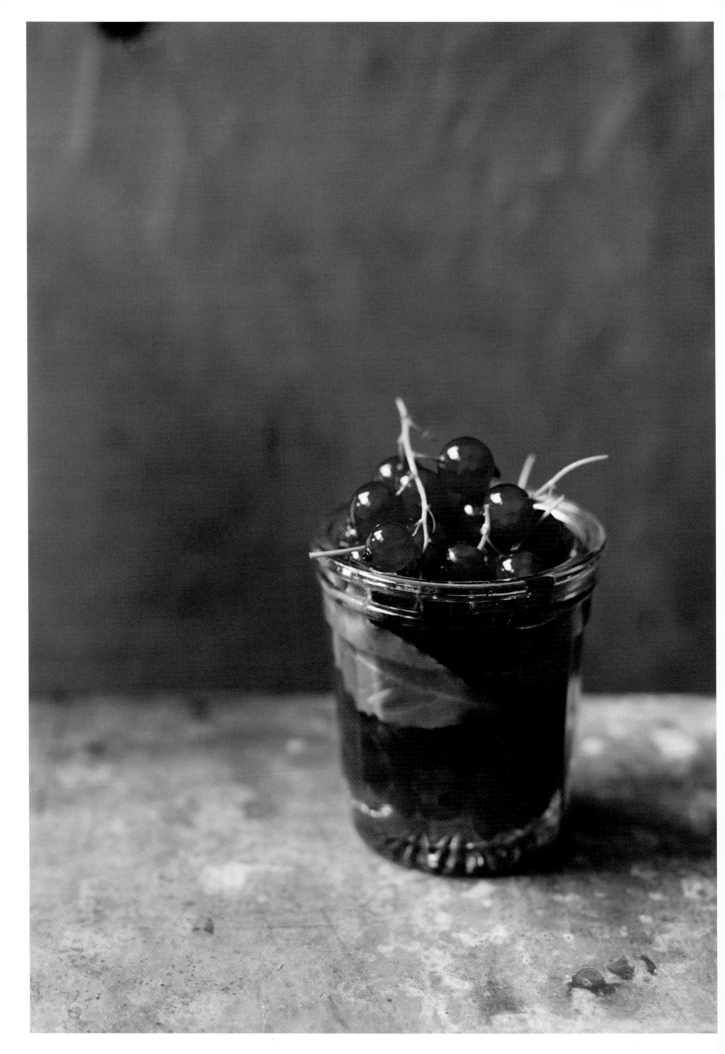

Pickled Redcurrants

Serve these jewelled pickled redcurrants alongside hearty pâtés and cold cuts.

MAKES 2 JARS

350ML WHITE WINE VINEGAR

4 TABLESPOONS CASTER SUGAR

3 ALLSPICE BERRIES

2 CLOVES

1 BAY LEAF

300G REDCURRANTS

Equipment

2 X 450G JAM JARS

Bring the vinegar to the boil in a small stainless steel saucepan with the sugar, allspice and cloves. Add the bay leaf and simmer for 5 minutes, then remove from the heat and leave to cool.

Meanwhile, wash the redcurrants in cold running water and leave to dry either on a clean tea towel or kitchen paper.

Pack the fruit into two sterilised jars (see page 132) and pour over the cooled vinegar. Seal the jars and leave in a cool, dark place for about 4 weeks before serving. They will keep for about 3 months in a cool, dark cupboard. Once opened, store in the fridge for up to 3 months.

Lemon and Almond Roulade with Redcurrants and Raspberries

Just occasionally I do like a show-offy type of pudding, and when I do, a roulade fits the bill nicely. The almonds, both ground and flaked, give this sponge a delicate flavour, sophisticated air and lightness, while the sharpness of the redcurrants cuts through the richness of the cream. And crisp, sugar-frosted strands of redcurrants – although somewhat retro – complete the picture. Although I've often served this roulade as a dessert on a summer's day, it wouldn't be out of place at a fancy afternoon tea.

SERVES 6–8

25G UNSALTED BUTTER, MELTED AND SLIGHTLY COOLED, PLUS EXTRA, MELTED, FOR GREASING

5 MEDIUM EGGS

125G CASTER SUGAR, PLUS 3 TABLESPOONS

FINELY GRATED ZEST OF ½ UNWAXED LEMON

75G PLAIN FLOUR, PLUS EXTRA FOR DUSTING

1 TEASPOON BAKING POWDER

75G GROUND ALMONDS

A PINCH OF SALT

50G FLAKED ALMONDS

For the filling

250G REDCURRANTS

1 TABLESPOON CASTER SUGAR

300ML DOUBLE CREAM

150G RASPBERRIES, PLUS EXTRA TO DECORATE

ICING SUGAR, FOR DUSTING

For the frosted redcurrants

200G REDCURRANTS IN CLUSTERS

1 MEDIUM EGG WHITE LIGHTLY BEATEN WITH 1 TEASPOON COLD WATER

150G CASTER SUGAR

Equipment

30 x 40CM SWISS ROLL TIN

Preheat the oven to 180°C/gas mark 4. Grease the tin with melted butter and line the base and sides with a large sheet of baking parchment. Grease the parchment and lightly dust with flour, tapping out the excess.

Using a free-standing mixer fitted with the whisk attachment, whisk the eggs and the 125g of caster sugar until very thick and pale, trebled in volume and the mixture leaves a ribbon trail when the whisk is lifted from the bowl. Add the lemon zest and sift in all the dry ingredients, except the flaked almonds, then, using a large metal spoon and a figure-of-eight action, gently fold in. Pour the melted butter around the edge of the bowl and fold in.

Gently pour into the prepared tin, spread level and scatter with the flaked almonds. Bake on the middle shelf of the oven for about 12 minutes until golden and just firm to touch. Meanwhile, lay a large sheet of baking parchment on the work surface and sprinkle it with the remaining 3 tablespoons of caster sugar.

Leave the baked sponge to rest for a minute before turning out onto the sugared parchment – this takes a leap of faith, but you simply hold the tin at both ends and flip it out in one quick movement. Carefully peel off the lining paper and then roll up the sponge, starting from the shortest end and with the clean parchment rolled inside the sponge. Leave to cool completely.

For the filling, strip the redcurrants from the stalks, place in a saucepan with the sugar and cook over a medium heat until they have burst. Continue to cook, stirring frequently, until thickened to a purée with the consistency of a soft-set jam. Remove from the heat and cool.

For the frosted redcurrants, using a small clean brush, paint the redcurrant clusters with the egg white solution and then sprinkle evenly and thickly with the sugar. Leave to dry on a wire rack.

Whip the cream into soft, pillowy peaks. Unroll the sponge and spread the surface evenly with the redcurrant purée. Using a palette knife, spread the cream on top, leaving a 2cm border all around the edge. Scatter with the raspberries, lightly crushing them in your fingers as you do so. Re-roll the roulade as tightly as possible, using the parchment to help you lift and roll. Carefully slide onto a serving plate, dust with icing sugar and decorate with the frosted redcurrants and extra raspberries.

Peach and Blackcurrant Pie

My mother makes a stunning peach and blackcurrant compote that she often serves with her famous meringues and a jug of cold pouring cream. It will forever remind me of lazy summer lunches in her colourful garden sitting under a large parasol. She also makes a mean fruit pie, so I've combined the two here to make what I think is something rather special. If you can't get hold of fresh blackcurrants you could use blueberries at a pinch, but they won't have the tartness of blackcurrants, so go easy on the sugar. Serve this pie warm with cold cream or scoops of vanilla ice cream.

SERVES 8

For the pastry

300G PLAIN FLOUR, PLUS EXTRA FOR DUSTING

A GOOD PINCH OF SEA SALT

180G UNSALTED BUTTER, DICED AND CHILLED

40G CASTER SUGAR, PLUS EXTRA FOR SPRINKLING

3 TABLESPOONS ICED WATER

2 TEASPOONS CIDER VINEGAR OR LEMON JUICE

½ MEDIUM EGG WHITE, LIGHTLY BEATEN

For the filling

4 LARGE RIPE PEACHES, WASHED, AND EACH CUT INTO 6 WEDGES

200G BLACKCURRANTS

2–3 TABLESPOONS CASTER SUGAR

FINELY GRATED ZEST OF ½ UNWAXED LEMON

1 ROUNDED TABLESPOON CORNFLOUR

20G UNSALTED BUTTER

Equipment

20–22CM DEEP PIE DISH OR OVEN PROOF SKILLET

Start by making the pastry. Tip the flour into a large mixing bowl, add the salt and butter and, using a round-bladed knife, cut the butter into the flour so that it starts to be rubbed into the flour. Use your fingers to continue rubbing the butter into the flour, lifting the mixture up out of the bowl and letting it almost roll over your fingertips. Be careful not to overwork – the butter should be incorporated into the flour with a few flecks still visible. Mix in the sugar with the knife.

Combine the iced water and vinegar or lemon juice in a cup and add two-thirds to the bowl. Mix in with the knife until the pastry starts to come together, adding more if necessary. Gather the dough together, trying not to knead it, and shape into a ball. Flatten into a disc, cover with clingfilm and chill for a good 2 hours.

Cut off one-third of the dough, cover and refrigerate until needed. Roll out the larger piece on a lightly floured work surface into a disc 28–30cm in diameter. Carefully roll it around the rolling pin and then unroll into the pie dish so that it covers the base and sides evenly, with a little excess draped over the sides. Without stretching the dough, press it into the corners. Using a sharp knife, trim off any excess, gather into a ball and save for the lattice. Chill for 20 minutes while you prepare the filling and preheat the oven to 170°C/gas mark 3. Place a baking tray on the middle shelf while the oven heats up.

Gently mix all the filling ingredients, except the butter, in a bowl without breaking up the fruit. Spoon into the pastry case and dot the filling with butter.

Dust the work surface with a little flour and roll out half the reserved pastry into a disc slightly larger than the top of the pie. Cut into 12 x 1cm-wide strips and arrange in a lattice over the fruit. Trim off any excess pastry, gather into a ball with the offcuts and roll out to a strip 6cm wide and about 50cm long. Cut into 3 x 1cm-wide strips and carefully plait together. Brush the top edge of the pie with water and lay the plait around it. Brush all the pastry with the beaten egg white, sprinkle with caster sugar and bake on the hot baking tray for 40–45 minutes until the filling is bubbling and the pastry golden brown

Blueberry and Lemon Verbena Buttermilk Sherbet

Blueberries and buttermilk are combined to make this light and refreshing frozen sherbet. If you prefer, you could use natural yogurt in place of buttermilk, and blackcurrants instead of blueberries. Lemon verbena is easy to grow in a pot. The sprigs and leaves can be used both fresh and dried for infusing syrups for fruit compotes or salads, and also make a wonderfully refreshing herbal tea.

SERVES 4–6

125G CASTER SUGAR, PLUS EXTRA IF NEEDED, TO TASTE

2 STRIPS OF PEEL FROM AN UNWAXED LEMON

SPRIG OF LEMON VERBENA

400G BLUEBERRIES

SQUEEZE OF LEMON JUICE, TO TASTE (OPTIONAL)

400ML BUTTERMILK

Equipment

FINE-MESH NYLON SIEVE

ICE-CREAM MAKER

PLASTIC FREEZER BOX

Tip the sugar into a medium saucepan and add the lemon peel strips, lemon verbena and 75ml cold water. Slowly bring to the boil to dissolve the sugar, then simmer for 30 seconds. Remove from the heat and leave to stand at room temperature for 1 hour or so for the lemon peel and lemon verbena to infuse the syrup.

Strain the syrup, return to the pan and bring back to the boil over a medium heat. Add the blueberries and simmer for about 3–4 minutes to soften the berries. Remove from the heat, scoop out one-third of the berries and reserve. Whizz the remainder to a purée using a stick blender. Pass the purée through a fine-mesh nylon sieve, pressing on the fruit to extract as much flavour and fruit as possible. Taste the purée and add a little more sugar or a squeeze of lemon juice to balance the flavours.

Add the buttermilk and the reserved berries and mix until thoroughly combined. Cover with clingfilm and chill in the fridge for 1 hour.

Churn the mixture in an ice-cream maker according to the manufacturer's instructions. Scoop the sherbet into a plastic freezer box, cover and freeze until firm before serving.

Blueberry and Almond Brioche Loaf

This is an impressive-looking loaf and one that is ideal to serve for brunch. You can prepare the first stage the night before and then simply assemble the loaf and leave it to rise the next morning. The method may seem rather long-winded, but I assure you it's simply a matter of plaiting the dough around the filling. As with most rich yeasted breads, this is best eaten on the day of making, but it will reheat quite happily the next day should you have leftovers.

SERVES 6–8

125ML FULL-FAT MILK, PLUS EXTRA FOR BRUSHING

40G UNSALTED BUTTER AT ROOM TEMPERATURE, DICED

250G STRONG WHITE FLOUR, PLUS EXTRA FOR DUSTING

5G FAST-ACTION/EASY-BLEND DRIED YEAST

25G CASTER SUGAR, PLUS 1–2 TABLESPOONS FOR SPRINKLING

A LARGE PINCH OF SALT

1 MEDIUM EGG, LIGHTLY BEATEN

SUNFLOWER OIL, FOR GREASING

200G BLUEBERRIES

1 MEDIUM EGG WHITE

For the frangipane

125G GROUND ALMONDS

75G UNSALTED BUTTER, SOFTENED

75G CASTER SUGAR

2 MEDIUM EGGS

25G PLAIN FLOUR

FINELY GRATED ZEST OF ½ UNWAXED LEMON

1 TEASPOON VANILLA EXTRACT

A PINCH OF SALT

Warm the milk until it's just a shade warmer than hand hot, add the butter and stir until melted. Thoroughly combine the flour, yeast, sugar and salt with a balloon whisk, before tipping everything into the bowl of a free-standing mixer fitted with a dough hook – this dough is quite soft and sticky, so it's easier to mix using a machine than by hand. Make a well in the middle of the dry ingredients and pour in the warm milk mixture. Add the beaten egg, mix well and knead on a medium speed for 5 minutes until silky smooth and elastic.

Shape the dough into a ball, place in a lightly oiled large mixing bowl and cover with clingfilm. Leave in a warm, draught-free place for 1½–2 hours or until doubled in size. Alternatively, prove overnight in the fridge.

Meanwhile, whizz all the frangipane ingredients in a food processor until smooth.

Lightly dust the work surface with flour and knead the dough for 30 seconds to knock out any air pockets. On a large sheet of baking parchment, roll the dough out into a rectangle 40 x 30cm and with one of the shorter sides closest to you. Mentally divide the dough into thirds from left to right and spread the frangipane into a neat, vertical rectangle in the middle third, leaving a 2–3cm border at the top and bottom. Scatter the blueberries evenly over the frangipane. Take a sharp knife and, starting on the right-hand third, cut the dough into 12 strips running slightly diagonally down from the edge of the filling outwards, leaving a 2–3cm rectangle top and bottom. Repeat on the left-hand side, ensuring that the strips are equal in number and width to those on the right-hand side. Brush the dough with a little milk and fold the top and bottom rectangles over to seal. Starting with the strip on the top left-hand side, fold it over to encase the filling, followed by the top right-hand strip. Repeat all the way down the loaf, overlapping each strip as you go.

Slide the loaf, still on the parchment, onto a large baking tray, loosely cover with oiled clingfilm and leave to rise in a warm place for 45 minutes–1 hour or until almost doubled in size again.

Preheat the oven to 180°C/gas mark 4. Beat the egg white until foamy, gently brush over the bread and scatter with caster sugar. Bake on the middle shelf for 20 minutes, then reduce the temperature to 170°C/gas mark 3 and cook for a further 10–15 minutes or until golden brown and well risen. You may need to turn the tray around in the oven halfway through baking to ensure that the loaf browns evenly. Remove from the oven and cool on a wire rack.

Blueberry Pies

The pastry in these individual pies is homemade puff pastry, which I am fully aware will have many people running for the chilled pastry section of the supermarket to seek out ready-made. I urge you to try homemade – it's far more delicious than anything from a packet and made in a factory. And as the filling is very simple, your time can be wisely spent on making the pastry. You could also fill the pies with small, ripe cherries, a mixture of apples and blackberries, or peaches and blackcurrants.

MAKES 6 PIES

1 QUANTITY OF PUFF PASTRY DOUGH
(SEE PAGE 207)

PLAIN FLOUR, FOR DUSTING

MILK, FOR BRUSHING

For the filling

400G BLUEBERRIES

2–3 TABLESPOONS CASTER SUGAR, PLUS
EXTRA FOR SPRINKLING

FINELY GRATED ZEST AND JUICE OF
½ UNWAXED LEMON

1 DESSERTPOON CORNFLOUR

Equipment

6 X 12CM ROUND INDIVIDUAL TART TINS

For the filling, tip half the blueberries into a small saucepan and add 1 tablespoon of the sugar and the lemon zest and juice. Cook over a low–medium heat for about 3 minutes until the blueberries have started to burst and become juicy. Remove from the heat and add the remaining blueberries, the cornflour and the remaining 1–2 tablespoons of sugar to taste, then leave to cool.

Dust the work surface with flour and divide the pastry dough into thirds. Divide one-third of the pastry into three even-sized pieces and roll each out into a circle, 2mm thick. Line three of the tart tins with the pastry, then use another third of the pastry to line the remaining three tins. Spoon the blueberry filling evenly between the pastry cases.

For the pastry lids, divide the last third of pastry into six even portions and roll each out into a circle, 2mm thick. Brush the inside edge of each pastry case with a little milk or water and place one lid on each pie, pressing the edges to seal. Using a sharp knife, trim off any excess pastry and use the back of the knife to crimp and knock up the edges of the pastry. Brush the tops with a little more milk and chill in the fridge for 30 minutes.

Preheat the oven to 180°C/gas mark 4 and place a solid baking tray on the middle shelf. Brush the tops of the tarts once again with milk and sprinkle with caster sugar. Cut a small cross in the middle of each pie top and bake on the hot baking tray for 30 minutes until the pastry is puffed and golden and the filling bubbling.

Leave the tarts to cool in the tins for 15–20 minutes and then serve warm with lashings of cream or ice cream.

Berries with Rose, Cardamom and Black Pepper Syrup

Dried rose petals are now widely available in larger supermarkets, online or in Middle Eastern grocers. However, if you happen to grow deeply scented roses in your garden then a handful of petals – fresh or dried – would be a really rather lovely addition to this fruit compote. As always when using fresh flowers, ensure that they are clean, bug-free and not sprayed with chemicals.

Homemade vanilla ice cream or a bowl of crème fraîche, Greek yogurt or softly whipped double cream would be perfect alongside this dessert.

SERVES 4–6

125G CASTER SUGAR

A GOOD PINCH OF DRIED ROSE PETALS (FOOD GRADE)

½ TEASPOON BLACK PEPPERCORNS

3 CARDAMOM PODS

JUICE OF ½ LEMON

400G STRAWBERRIES

150G REDCURRANTS

300G RASPBERRIES

5 FRESH FIGS, WASHED

Tip the sugar into a saucepan, add 200ml of cold water and the rose petals. Using a pestle and mortar, very lightly crush the black peppercorns and cardamom pods and add to the pan. Set the pan over a low-medium heat to gently dissolve the sugar. Bring to the boil, reduce to a simmer and continue to cook gently for 2 minutes. Remove the syrup from the heat, add the lemon juice and leave to cool and infuse with the petals and spices for 2 hours.

Hull and halve the strawberries and tip into a serving bowl. Using a fork, strip the redcurrants from their stems directly into the bowl. Add the raspberries and figs, cut into slim wedges. Strain the syrup over the fruit, stir gently to combine and leave for 30 minutes to 1 hour to allow the flavours to mingle before serving.

Seedless Raspberry Jelly

With its intense raspberry flavour and ruby-like shimmer, this jelly is not your everyday kind of spread. In fact, this would be just the thing to slather on top of the finest crumpets or scones for visiting VIP guests or royalty. And because it's rather special, this recipe doesn't make many jars. As well as a topping for scones, it makes a good filling for cakes, nutty or chocolate shortbreads or macarons.

MAKES 4 JARS

650G RASPBERRIES

400G JAM SUGAR

JUICE OF ½ LEMON

Equipment

STAINLESS STEEL PRESERVING PAN

JELLY BAG OR LARGE PIECE OF CLEAN MUSLIN

4 x 250G JAM JARS

If you don't already own a jelly bag, then I urge you to invest in one. They are relatively inexpensive, and once you're got the bug for making jellies and the like, you'll be hooked. I've used jam sugar for this recipe, which has a small amount of pectin already added, but if you can't find any, simply use granulated sugar and add a small handful of fresh redcurrants at the start of the recipe – they have a high pectin content that will help speed up the setting process.

Tip the raspberries and 150ml water into the pan and gently warm over a low heat until the berries have broken down and released lots of scarlet-coloured juice. Press and crush the fruit against the sides of the pan with a wooden spoon to encourage this process along, but don't allow the berries and juice to boil at this stage, as you want to preserve the fresh, vibrant raspberry flavour and colour.

Tip the contents of the pan into a jelly bag (or large piece of clean muslin draped over a fine-mesh sieve) and suspend the bag over a clean bowl. I tie the loops of the jelly bag around the handles of a kitchen cupboard to get some elevation over the bowl. Leave the juice to drip slowly through the bag for at least 4 hours, but better still overnight. Don't be tempted to push, prod, squeeze or poke the fruit, otherwise you'll end up with a cloudy juice that will produce a seedless jam rather than a crystal clear jelly. Once all of the juice has dripped through the bag you will be left with a bowl of scarlet juice and a jelly bag of raspberry pulp. Discard the pulp.

Preheat the oven to 150°C/gas mark 2. Measure the juice – you should have about 500ml, but if you have less, make up the quantity with water. Pour into a clean saucepan, add the sugar and a tablespoon of the lemon juice and bring slowly to the boil, stirring to completely dissolve the sugar. Cook at a steady boil for about 10 minutes, removing any scum that rises to the top of the juice with a slotted spoon, and then start testing to see if the jelly has reached setting point. Drop a teaspoonful of mixture onto a chilled saucer, leave it for 30 seconds–1 minute and then push it with the tip of your finger. If the jelly wrinkles, it's ready; if not, cook for a further 3 minutes and then test for a set again.

Slide the pan off the heat, taste the jelly and add a drop more lemon juice to sharpen the flavour if needed and remove any scum that might have formed. Ladle the jelly into a jug and then pour into hot, sterilised jars (see page 132). Screw on the lids and leave until completely cold before labelling and storing and in a cool, dark cupboard for up to 1 year. Once opened, store the jelly in the fridge and use within 1 month.

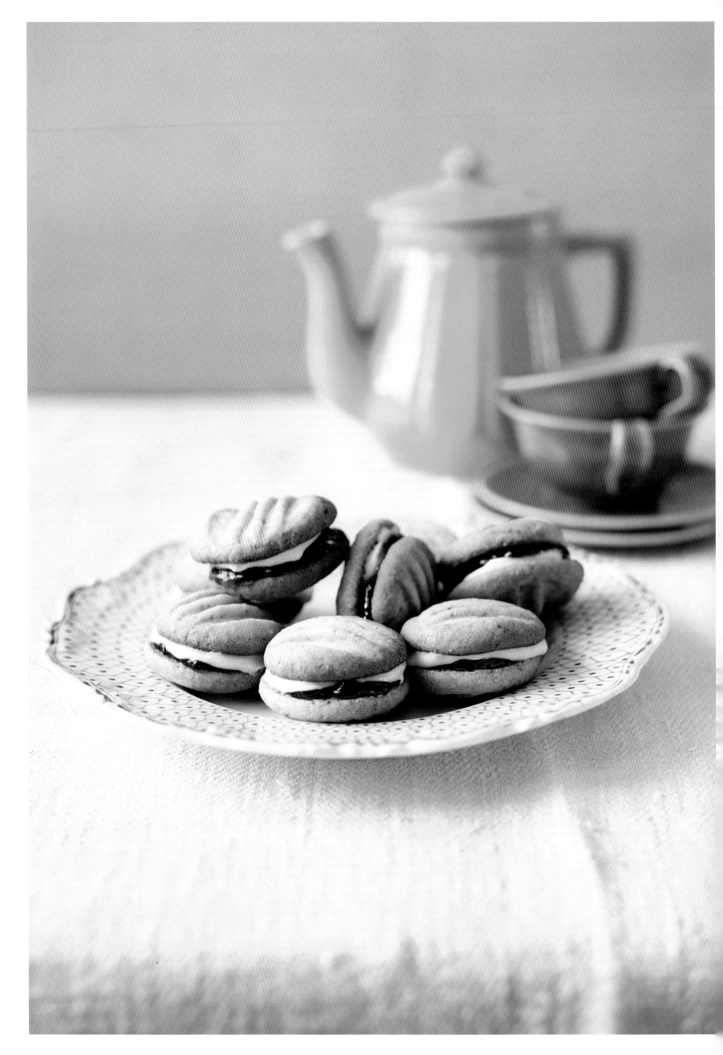

Raspberry, Pistachio and Passion Fruit Yo-Yos

As a child, I used to love a particular brand of jam sandwich cookies – they were filled with white buttercream and jam and each cookie had a smiley face imprinted on the surface. These are a more sophisticated spin on those old childhood favourites and are a perfect use for my Seedless Raspberry Jelly (see page 96).

MAKES 20

For the cookies

50G SHELLED UNSALTED PISTACHIOS

175G UNSALTED BUTTER, SOFTENED

75G ICING SUGAR

200G PLAIN FLOUR

½ TEASPOON BAKING POWDER

50G CORNFLOUR

A PINCH OF SALT

2 TABLESPOONS SIEVED PASSION FRUIT JUICE OR MILK

For the filling

75G WHITE CHOCOLATE, CHOPPED

75G UNSALTED BUTTER, SOFTENED

150G ICING SUGAR

2 PASSION FRUIT, HALVED WITH SEEDS AND PULP SCOOPED OUT

20 TEASPOONS SEEDLESS RASPBERRY JELLY (SEE PAGE 96)

Preheat the oven to 170°C/gas mark 3 and line two baking trays with baking parchment.

Make the cookies first. Very finely chop the pistachios – you will find this easier and quicker if you have a mini chopper, or whizz in a food processor. Cream the butter and icing sugar until very pale and fluffy – this will take about 4 minutes using a free-standing mixer. Sift in the dry ingredients, add the chopped pistachios and passion fruit juice or milk and mix well until smooth.

Break off large, cherry-sized nuggets of dough, roll into smooth balls and arrange on the prepared baking trays – you should have 40 balls. Dip the tines of a fork into cold water and firmly press into the top of each cookie to flatten slightly (the water helps to stop the dough sticking to the tines). Bake on the middle shelf of the oven for about 12 minutes until pale golden, swapping the trays around halfway through the baking time to ensure that they colour evenly. Leave to cool on the trays.

To make the filling, melt the chocolate in a heatproof bowl, either in the microwave in short bursts on a low setting or over a saucepan of barely simmering water. Stir until smooth and leave to cool slightly.

Cream the butter and icing sugar until smooth, pale and light. Add the passion fruit and melted chocolate and beat until smooth and spreadable.

Spread the underside of 20 of the cookies with a teaspoon of filling and the remaining cookies with the raspberry jelly. Sandwich the two together and serve with a smile!

Raspberry Tarts

Elegant enough to be served at the most fancy afternoon tea party, these little tartlets have a double hit of raspberry. The filling is a rich raspberry custard, which is then topped with a layer of Seedless Raspberry Jelly (see page 96). But if you don't have the inclination to make the jelly, a good raspberry jam will suffice.

MAKES 12

For the pastry

200g PLAIN FLOUR, PLUS EXTRA FOR DUSTING

40g ICING SUGAR, PLUS EXTRA FOR DUSTING

A PINCH OF SALT

125g UNSALTED BUTTER, CHILLED AND DICED

1 MEDIUM EGG YOLK

2 TABLESPOONS ICED WATER

2 TEASPOONS LEMON JUICE

For the filling

350g RASPBERRIES, PLUS EXTRA TO SERVE

100–125g CASTER SUGAR, PLUS 2 TABLESPOONS

SQUEEZE OF LEMON JUICE

1 MEDIUM EGG

3 MEDIUM EGG YOLKS

125ML DOUBLE CREAM OR CRÈME FRAÎCHE

To serve

6 TABLESPOONS Seedless Raspberry Jelly (SEE PAGE 96)

CRÈME FRAÎCHE

EDIBLE FLOWERS

Equipment

FINE-MESH NYLON SIEVE

12 TARTLET TINS

12CM PLAIN COOKIE CUTTER

Tip the flour into the bowl of a food processor, add the icing sugar and salt and pulse briefly to combine. Then add the butter and pulse briefly again until just incorporated. Tip the mixture into a mixing bowl and make a well in the middle. Add the egg yolk, iced water and lemon juice and, using a round-bladed bread-and-butter knife, cut through the mixture to combine the ingredients and bring the dough together. Use your hands to very lightly knead the dough and to form it into a neat ball, but try not to overwork the dough or the resulting pastry will be tough rather than light and crumbly. Flatten the dough into a disc, cover with clingfilm and chill in the fridge for 2 hours.

Next, make the filling. Place the raspberries in a small saucepan with the 2 tablespoons caster sugar and a splash of water. Cook over a low heat for about 6 minutes until the fruit is very soft and the purée just starts to thicken. Push through a fine-mesh nylon sieve into a bowl. Add the remaining sugar, the quantity depending on how naturally sweet the purée is, and leave to cool for 10 minutes. Beat the whole egg and egg yolks together and add to the purée with the cream or crème fraîche and whisk to combine. Strain through the sieve into a bowl and set aside.

Lightly dust the work surface with flour and roll the pastry out to a thickness of no more than 2mm. Stamp out discs from the pastry with the cutter and use to line the tartlet tins, pressing the pastry into the corners. Prick the bases and chill the tart cases in the fridge for 15 minutes while you preheat the oven to 170°C/gas mark 3. Line each tart case with foil and fill with baking beans or uncooked rice, arrange on a baking tray and bake on the middle shelf of the oven for 10–12 minutes until pale golden. Remove the foil and baking beans or rice and divide the filling between the tart cases. Return to the oven for a further 12–13 minutes until the filling has set. Leave until completely cold and then chill in the fridge until firm.

Warm the raspberry jelly in a small saucepan and brush over the top of each tart. Decorate the tarts with a small dollop of crème fraîche, extra raspberries, edible flowers and a light dusting of icing sugar.

Summer Berry Tiramisu Cake

This is a real show-stopper cake – something to make for an occasion when you have a little time and berries and currants are plentiful. It's not tricky to make but does require concentration – and a crowd to feed. The filling is a twist on zabaglione, which on its own would be delicious – even without the mascarpone and white chocolate – served warm over macerated berries or sliced peaches. I have chosen to make this cake an impressive six-layered affair, but it can just as easily be left as a more manageable three tiers. You may have some filling left over, which can be served alongside.

SERVES 8–10

For the cake layers

50G UNSALTED BUTTER, MELTED AND SLIGHTLY COOLED, PLUS EXTRA FOR GREASING

6 LARGE EGGS

150G CASTER SUGAR

1 TEASPOON VANILLA EXTRACT

150G PLAIN FLOUR, PLUS EXTRA FOR DUSTING

50G GROUND ALMONDS

1 TEASPOON BAKING POWDER

A PINCH OF SALT

For the mascarpone filling

4 LARGE EGG YOLKS

50G CASTER SUGAR

2 TABLESPOONS Marsala

A PINCH OF SALT

FINELY GRATED ZEST OF 1 LEMON

500G MASCARPONE, BEATEN UNTIL SMOOTH

100G WHITE CHOCOLATE, CHOPPED AND MELTED

For the macerated berries

750G MIXED BERRIES AND CURRANTS, PLUS EXTRA TO SERVE

1 TABLESPOON LEMON JUICE

1 TABLESPOON CASTER SUGAR

½ TEASPOON VANILLA EXTRACT

3 TABLESPOONS Marsala

ICING SUGAR, FOR DUSTING

Equipment

3 x 20CM SANDWICH CAKE TINS

Preheat the oven to 180°C/gas mark 4. Grease the inside of the cake tins and line the bases with discs of greased baking parchment. Lightly dust the insides of the tins with flour and tap out the excess.

Using a free-standing mixer fitted with a whisk attachment, whisk the eggs, sugar and vanilla together on medium-high speed until very thick and pale, trebled in volume and the mixture leaves a ribbon trail when the whisk is lifted from the bowl. Sift in the dry ingredients and, using a large metal spoon, gently fold in. Pour the melted butter around the edge of the bowl and gently fold in.

Divide the batter evenly between the prepared tins – I carefully weigh the mixture to ensure that my cakes are 100% even – spread level and bake on the middle shelf of the oven for 18–20 minutes or until golden, well risen and a wooden skewer inserted into the middle comes out clean. Leave to cool in the tins for a couple of minutes, then lift out onto a wire rack to cool completely.

For the filling, whisk the egg yolks, sugar, Marsala and salt in a heatproof glass or ceramic bowl set over a saucepan of simmering water. Continue whisking for 5 minutes or until the mixture is hot to the touch, very thick, tripled in volume and the consistency of softly whipped cream. Remove from the heat and plunge the base of the bowl into cold water to cool, add the lemon zest and whisk until cold. Fold in the mascarpone and melted chocolate.

Place the berries, lemon juice, sugar and vanilla in a bowl and stir to coat. Leave to macerate for 10 minutes.

Using a bread knife, slice each cake in half horizontally. Choose the best-looking top slice and set aside. Lay the remaining slices on the work surface and drizzle with the Marsala. Divide the filling between the slices, spreading it almost to the edge. Place one of the bottom layers on a serving plate and scatter with one-fifth of the berries. Top with a second layer and more berries. Continue layering in this manner, finishing with the reserved layer. Gently press the layers together, cover loosely with clingfilm and chill for 1 hour. Serve with a pile of extra berries on top and a light dusting of icing sugar.

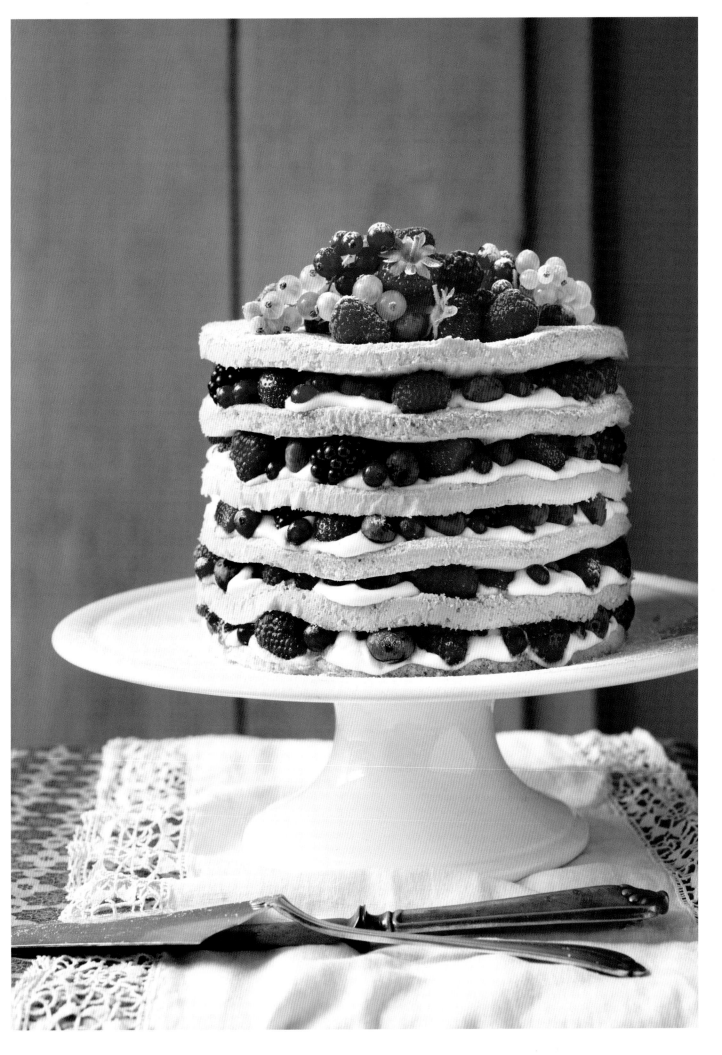

Summer Berry Trifles

This elegant pudding has all the classic elements of a trifle but assembled in a looser, free-form fashion. Although this recipe has a number of stages, each part can be prepared in advance and plated just before serving.

SERVES 6

For the jelly

250G HULLED STRAWBERRIES, SLICED

200G RASPBERRIES

2 TABLESPOONS CASTER SUGAR, PLUS EXTRA TO TASTE

A SQUEEZE OF LEMON JUICE

2 LEAVES OF PLATINUM-GRADE LEAF GELATINE

For the cake

3 MEDIUM EGGS

100G CASTER SUGAR

1 TEASPOON FINELY GRATED LEMON ZEST

50G PLAIN FLOUR, PLUS EXTRA FOR DUSTING

50G GROUND ALMONDS

1 TEASPOON BAKING POWDER

A PINCH OF SALT

40G UNSALTED BUTTER, MELTED AND SLIGHTLY COOLED, PLUS EXTRA FOR GREASING

8 TEASPOONS SEEDLESS RASPBERRY JELLY (SEE PAGE 96) OR RASPBERRY JAM

For the custard

200ML FULL-FAT MILK

75G CASTER SUGAR

3 LARGE EGG YOLKS

1 LEVEL TABLESPOON CORNFLOUR

1 TEASPOON VANILLA BEAN PASTE

200ML DOUBLE CREAM, WHIPPED UNTIL THICK BUT STILL FLOPPY

For the berries

75G CASTER SUGAR

1 TABLESPOON FOOD-GRADE DRIED ROSE PETALS OR 1 TEASPOON ROSEWATER

A GOOD SQUEEZE OF LEMON JUICE

200G RASPBERRIES

100G BLUEBERRIES

200G STRAWBERRIES, HULLED AND QUARTERED

Equipment

14 x 20CM TRAY OR PLASTIC FREEZER BOX LINED WITH CLINGFILM

30 x 40CM SWISS ROLL OR BAKING TIN

4–5CM PLAIN COOKIE CUTTER

For the jelly, heat the berries, sugar, lemon juice and 4 tablespoons of cold water in a saucepan over a low heat to dissolve the sugar and soften the fruit. Continue to heat gently for 10 minutes or until the berries completely break down and release their juices. Pour into a fine-mesh nylon sieve over a bowl and leave the juice to drip through, without pressing the fruit – this can take up to 4 hours. Measure the juice – you should have about 250ml – and add enough water to make up to 300ml. Taste and add more sugar if needed.

Soak the gelatine leaves in a bowl of cold water for 10 minutes until soft. Heat half the berry juice in a small saucepan to just below boiling, then remove from the heat. Drain the gelatine leaves, squeeze out any excess water, add to the hot juice and whisk to combine. Add the remaining juice, whisk again and pour into the clingfilm-lined tray or box. Leave to cool, then cover and chill in the fridge for at least 2 hours until set.

Meanwhile, preheat the oven to 180°C/gas mark 4. Line the baking tin with greased baking parchment, lightly dust with flour and tap out the excess. Using a free-standing mixer fitted with a whisk attachment, whisk the eggs and sugar until thick, pale and doubled in volume. Add the lemon zest and whisk again. Sift in the dry ingredients and fold in using a large metal spoon. Pour the melted butter around the edge of the bowl and gently fold in. Carefully spoon into the prepared tin and spread level. Bake on the middle shelf for 9–10 minutes until golden and firm to the touch. Leave to cool in the tin.

Using the cookie cutter, stamp out 24 discs from the cake. Spread 12 with the raspberry jelly or jam and sandwich with the remaining discs.

For the custard, bring the milk to the boil in a saucepan. In a bowl, whisk together the sugar, egg yolks, cornflour and vanilla. Pour the hot milk over and whisk constantly until smooth and thoroughly combined. Return to the pan and cook gently, whisking constantly, until thickened and you can no longer taste the cornflour. Pour through a fine-mesh sieve into a clean bowl, cover the surface with clingfilm and leave until cold. Chill for at least 2 hours. Fold in the whipped cream.

For the berries, bring 75ml water, the sugar, rose petals or rosewater and lemon juice to the boil in a small pan until the sugar has dissolved, remove from the heat and leave to infuse for 1 hour. Strain into another pan, discarding the rose petals, if using, and bring back to the boil, then remove from the heat and add the berries. Leave to infuse for 1 hour.

To serve, turn the jelly out and cut into neat dice. Spoon 2 tablespoons of custard into each bowl, scatter with the diced jelly and arrange 2 little sandwich cakes to one side. Top with a spoonful of berries and a drizzle of rose-scented syrup and serve immediately.

Pistachio, Coconut and Lime Cake

This is one of my all-time favourite cakes – and that's saying something for a chocolate cake fiend! Serve it on the day of baking or make it the day ahead; either way, it's pretty darn good. There's just enough coconut for you to know it's there, but not so much that it overpowers the tangy lime and nutty pistachio. Drizzled with just enough syrup to moisten the cake without drowning it and making it heavy, and accompanied by gently softened, lime-infused berries and a spoonful of cool fromage frais or crème fraîche, it's just as good served as a pudding as it is with afternoon tea.

If you happen to find a bottle of pistachio oil in your local deli, then grab it and use it in this recipe. It has a wonderful nutty flavour and aroma that hits you the moment you unscrew the cap – it's pricey but can also be used to make a delicious pesto salad dressing (see page 147). I try also to use nibbed pistachios, which have had their purple skins removed. They are available from Middle Eastern supermarkets and specialist online food suppliers.

SERVES 8–10

For the cake

75G UNSALTED BUTTER, SOFTENED, PLUS
EXTRA FOR GREASING

75ML OLIVE OR PISTACHIO OIL

175G SHELLED UNSALTED PISTACHIOS

50G UNSWEETENED DESICCATED COCONUT

125G PLAIN FLOUR

2 TEASPOONS BAKING POWDER

A PINCH OF SALT

4 MEDIUM EGGS

225G CASTER SUGAR

FINELY GRATED ZEST OF 2 UNWAXED LIMES

3 ROUNDED TABLESPOONS SOURED CREAM

For the syrup

FRESHLY SQUEEZED JUICE OF 3 LIMES

5 TABLESPOONS AGAVE SYRUP OR MILD-
TASTING CLEAR HONEY

3 TABLESPOONS CASTER SUGAR

200G BLUEBERRIES

200G BLACKBERRIES

NATURAL FROMAGE FRAIS, CRÈME FRAÎCHE
OR GREEK YOGURT, TO SERVE

Equipment

23CM SPRINGFORM CAKE TIN

Preheat the oven to 170C°/gas mark 3. Grease the tin and line the base with baking parchment.

Melt the butter with the olive or pistachio oil in a small saucepan over a low heat. Remove from the heat and leave to cool slightly.

Whizz the pistachios in a food processor until they are very finely chopped. Add the coconut, flour, baking powder and salt and whizz for no more than 10 seconds, just to combine.

Using an electric mixer, whisk the eggs and sugar on medium–high speed until they are very thick and pale, trebled in volume and leave a ribbon trail when the whisk is lifted from the bowl. Gently fold in the lime zest and pistachio mixture using a large metal spoon, then fold in the butter mixture and soured cream. Pour into the tin, spread level and bake on the middle shelf of the oven for 40–50 minutes or until a wooden skewer inserted into the middle comes out clean.

Meanwhile, prepare the syrup. In a small saucepan, bring the lime juice, agave syrup or honey, sugar and 200ml of cold water to the boil. Continue to bubble steadily until reduced by half and syrupy.

Leave the cake to cool in the tin on a wire rack for 5 minutes, then carefully run an off-set palette knife around the edge of the cake to release the sides from the tin. Using the wooden skewer, make holes all over the top of the cake, then while it is still in the tin either slowly drizzle or carefully brush half the syrup all over the warm cake. Set aside until completely cold.

Tip the berries into the remaining syrup and return to a low heat for a couple of minutes to slightly soften them. Remove from the heat, spoon into a bowl and leave to cool.

Serve the cake in slices with fromage frais, crème fraîche or Greek yogurt and the berry compote spooned over.

Stone

As summer rolls along, nature provides us with yet another staggering array of fruits, with cherries, peaches, nectarines, plums and apricots being possibly my best loved of all. As delicious eaten raw as they are cooked, and shining in both savoury and sweet dishes, stone fruits earn their rightful place in my kitchen and cooking, whether in salads and bakes, drinks and preserves or in decadent ice creams and refreshing ice pops and sorbets.

A bag of fully ripe, glistening dark purple cherries is like a bag of treasure. If you are anything like me and you're cooking a dish that calls for fresh cherries, you'll need to buy twice as many as the recipe requires, as they are impossible to resist. I will certainly have eaten handfuls before getting anywhere near the kitchen.

As high summer kicks in, so does the peach and nectarine season. Peaches – yellow or white-fleshed, round or doughnut-shaped – are one of those fruits that I seem to almost overdose on during the summer months. I spent years living in South West France where we had a small peach tree in the garden, but size was not an issue when it came to the quantity of fruit that this one modest tree yielded. As all of some 200 peaches ripened in a couple of weeks, we cooked up jams, preserves, syrups and chutneys to make the most of the crop and not waste a single fruit. I still adore large yellow-fleshed peaches despite the fruit frenzy that I associate with them.

Perfect apricots with their slightly downy skin and shape that makes me think of an angel's bottom seem to come to life when cooked – even less-than-perfect apricots can be transformed with a little heat and sugar. The same applies to plums – even slightly under-ripe specimens when cut in half, sprinkled with sugar and baked in a moderate oven become a delicious affair that can be served straight up or puréed and churned in an ice-cream maker for one of my favourite sorbets.

All varieties of stone fruit make wonderful jams and preserves. I prefer my jam slightly less sweet than is traditional, resulting in a slightly softer set and shorter shelf life, but this allows the bright flavour of the fruit to really shine through. I also make jams in smaller batches, which is partly due to my desire to make the most of the season's offerings and variety, but also so that I can fill my cupboards with a wider selection of flavours without feeling overwhelmed by a half hundredweight of one type.

Bulgar Wheat Salad with Cherries and Feta

This is the kind of food that I love most – fresh and full of flavour. It's ideal for those lazy outdoor summer lunches, when you really don't fancy standing in a hot kitchen for longer than necessary. And it tastes even better the next day. Serve with Lamb Kofte (see page 114), simply barbecued lamb chops or a za'atar-crusted rack of lamb or fish – or just with some warm flatbreads and a bowl of hummus.

SERVES 4–6

250G BULGAR WHEAT

50G WHOLE ALMONDS

50G FLAT-LEAF PARSLEY

30G FRESH MINT

30G FRESH CORIANDER

50G ROCKET

1 HEAD OF FENNEL

5 SPRING ONIONS

A HANDFUL OF RADISHES

1 SMALL LEBANESE CUCUMBER OR
½ REGULAR CUCUMBER

JUICE OF 1 LEMON, OR TO TASTE

4–5 TABLESPOONS FRUITY OLIVE OIL,
OR TO TASTE

250G CHERRIES, WASHED AND DRIED

150G FETA

A GOOD PINCH OF GROUND SUMAC
(OPTIONAL)

SALT AND FRESHLY GROUND BLACK PEPPER

Wash the bulgar wheat in a sieve under cold running water. Tip into a pan, cover with 1 litre of cold water and add a pinch of salt. Bring to the boil, half cover and simmer for about 15 minutes until tender. Drain and refresh under cold running water. Leave to drain in the sieve while you prepare the remaining ingredients.

Toast the almonds either in a dry frying pan over a medium heat – shaking the pan to prevent the nuts from scorching – or in the oven on a baking tray for 3–4 minutes if you happen to have it on already. When cool enough to handle, cut into slivers.

Chop the parsley, mint, coriander and rocket – how fine you chop the herbs depends on your preference, but I usually go for roughly chopped – and tip into a large bowl. Trim the fennel, cut into quarters through the root and cut out the tough core from each wedge. Finely slice and add to the herbs. Trim and finely chop the spring onions. Wash and trim the radishes and finely slice or cut into matchsticks. Wash the cucumber, trim the ends and cut into small dice. Add all to the bowl.

Squeeze out any remaining water from the bulgar wheat and tip into the bowl. Add the lemon juice and olive oil, season well with salt and black pepper and mix to combine.

Now for the cherries. Taking one at a time, remove the stalk and, holding it over the salad bowl, squeeze it between your fingers to pop out the stone – this way, the cherry juice drips into the salad and isn't wasted. Break the cherry flesh into rough pieces and add to the bowl. Crumble the feta over the top, add the almonds and mix gently to combine.

This salad tastes best an hour or so after making, once all the flavours have mingled. After this time, taste the salad and add more oil, lemon juice, salt or pepper if needed. Sprinkle with the sumac, if using, and serve.

Lamb Kofte with Cherries

I love simple, super-tasty dishes that are perfect for sharing. These little meatballs make an ideal light lunch, or can be served as part of a bigger spread and would be wonderful with my Bulgar Wheat Salad with Cherries and Feta on page 112. Here, these kofte are served with chargrilled flatbreads, snappy pickled red onion, pickled green chillies, a cooling tahini sauce and fresh cucumbers. But as an alternative, try adding a can of good-quality chopped tomatoes to the pan of browned kofte, enough stock to just cover and a dash of pomegranate molasses, then cover and cook for 30 minutes in a moderate oven.

SERVES 4

2 TABLESPOONS OLIVE OIL

1 SMALL ONION, FINELY CHOPPED

1 FAT GARLIC CLOVE, FINELY CHOPPED

50G PINE NUTS

30G FLAT-LEAF PARSLEY, FINELY CHOPPED

30G FRESH MINT, FINELY CHOPPED

1 GREEN CHILLI, DESEEDED AND
FINELY CHOPPED

½ TEASPOON GROUND CUMIN

¼ TEASPOON GROUND ALLSPICE

¼ TEASPOON GROUND CINNAMON

150G CHERRIES, WASHED

400G LEAN LAMB MINCE

SALT AND FRESHLY GROUND BLACK PEPPER

For the pickled red onion

1 RED ONION, THINLY SLICED

2 TABLESPOONS WHITE WINE VINEGAR

2 TEASPOONS GOLDEN CASTER SUGAR

A PINCH OF SALT

For the tahini sauce

1 FAT GARLIC CLOVE, CRUSHED

2 TABLESPOONS TAHINI PASTE

4 TABLESPOONS GREEK YOGURT

JUICE OF ½ LEMON, OR TO TASTE

½ TEASPOON GROUND CUMIN

To serve

CHARGRILLED FLATBREADS

SMALL LEBANESE CUCUMBERS

PICKLED GREEN CHILLIES

LEMON WEDGES

Heat 1 tablespoon of the olive oil in a small saucepan, add the onion and cook gently for about 3 minutes until soft but not coloured. Add the garlic and cook for a further minute. Tip into a bowl. Lightly toast the pine nuts in the same pan, shaking them to ensure that they brown evenly without scorching, and add to the onion and garlic. Add the herbs and chilli to the bowl along with the spices. Remove the stalk from each cherry and, holding it over the bowl to catch any juices, squeeze it between your fingers to pop out the stone. Roughly chop the cherry flesh and add to the bowl with the lamb mince. Season well with salt and black pepper and, using your hands, mix and knead the mixture to thoroughly combine. Shape into neat golf ball-sized balls.

Preheat the oven to 190°C/gas mark 5. Heat the remaining tablespoon of olive oil in a frying pan over a medium heat and cook the kofte in batches for about 3 minutes, turning them frequently so that they brown well on all sides. Transfer to an ovenproof dish or tray and keep warm in the oven while you prepare the pickled red onion and the sauce.

Toss the red onion in a glass or ceramic bowl with the vinegar, sugar and salt and leave for 20 minutes to soften and lightly pickle. In a small bowl, mix together all the ingredients for the tahini sauce with enough water until smooth and the consistency of very softly whipped cream. Taste and add salt and/or more lemon juice to taste.

Serve the kofte hot with the pickled red onion, tahini sauce, chargrilled flatbreads, cucumber wedges, pickled green chillies and lemon wedges to squeeze over.

Cherry Cordial

Now here's a hard-working bottle of goodness. Not only does this cordial make deliciously refreshing soft drinks and ice pops when diluted with still or sparkling water, it can be stirred through yogurt, drizzled over pancakes and makes a mighty fine addition to that retro burger bar classic Coke Float: drop a scoop of vanilla ice cream into a tall glass, top up with Coca-Cola and a drizzle of cherry cordial. Or keep it simple and serve a generous slug of cordial over vanilla or chocolate ice cream. However, even better and for a more adult theme, try adding some to your summer cocktail experiments. A splash of cordial and a dash of cherry brandy will give some extra oomph to a glass of inferior sparkling wine. And if you were to thicken the syrup, soften the cherries and reduce the syrup a little further, it would be rather wonderful to spoon the warm syrup and sticky cherries over rich, dark chocolate brownies. Add a good dollop of softly whipped cream and I think I might be swooning.

MAKES ABOUT 600ML

750G CHERRIES, WASHED

½ VANILLA POD, SPLIT IN HALF LENGTHWAYS

350G CASTER SUGAR

JUICE OF ½ LEMON

Equipment

FINE-MESH NYLON SIEVE

2 X 330ML BOTTLES

ICE POP MOULDS (OPTIONAL)

Remove the stalk from each cherry and cut in half. Using your fingers, remove the stones and tip the fruit into a mixing bowl. This might seem a labour-intensive way to remove the stones but it's really quite satisfying. Add the vanilla pod to the bowl with the sugar and lemon juice. Stir well, cover and leave at room temperature for at least 1 hour to allow the sugar to completely dissolve and to draw the juice from the cherries.

Scoop the mixture into a saucepan, add 250ml cold water and place over a low heat. Bring to the boil and then simmer for 3–4 minutes. Pour through a fine-mesh nylon sieve into a jug and leave for a couple of hours for every last drop to drip through. Pour into sterilised bottles (see page 132), seal and store in the fridge until needed. It will keep for up to 6 weeks.

To make ice pops, dilute the cordial to taste and then add a drop more cordial – this instruction may seem contradictory, but as the cordial freezes it will lose a little sweetness and flavour, so you'll need to add a bit extra to compensate for this. Pour into ice pop moulds and freeze until solid. Perfect on a balmy summer's day.

You can also make this cordial using strawberries in place of cherries – add a handful of pineapple mint leaves for a further twist.

Cherry and Almond Crumble Cake

This cake has a number of elements that at first glance might look a little intimidating, but bear with me. It received a big thumbs-up from my harshest critic and chief taste tester who felt that all the various layers were necessary – and Mum knows best. On the bottom is a buttery shortbread base, topped with a layer of cherry jam, followed by a rich almond cake studded with fresh juicy cherries that are almost hidden under a crisp crumble topping. If you want to make life one little step easier, you could leave out the crumble layer and simply scatter the top of the cake with flaked or nibbed almonds. It's equally good served slightly warm as a pudding, with vanilla ice cream or cream.

SERVES 8–10

For the shortbread base

125G PLAIN FLOUR

100G UNSALTED BUTTER, CHILLED AND DICED, PLUS EXTRA FOR GREASING

40G ICING SUGAR

A PINCH OF SALT

3 TABLESPOONS CHERRY JAM

For the crumble topping

40G FLAKED ALMONDS

50G SOFT LIGHT BROWN SUGAR

40G PLAIN FLOUR

25G UNSALTED BUTTER, MELTED

For the cake

125G UNSALTED BUTTER, SOFTENED

125G CASTER SUGAR

3 MEDIUM EGGS, BEATEN

1 TEASPOON FINELY GRATED UNWAXED LEMON ZEST

1 TEASPOON VANILLA BEAN PASTE OR EXTRACT

¼ TEASPOON ALMOND EXTRACT

100G GROUND ALMONDS

75G PLAIN FLOUR

1 TEASPOON BAKING POWDER

A PINCH OF SALT

2 TABLESPOONS SOURED CREAM

350G CHERRIES, STONED

Equipment

20CM SPRINGFORM CAKE TIN

Preheat the oven to 180°C/gas mark 4. Grease the cake tin and line the base with baking parchment.

Prepare the shortbread base first. In a food processor, pulse together the flour, butter, icing sugar and salt until the butter has been rubbed into the flour. Tip into the prepared tin and press into an even layer covering the base. If your jam is a tad chunky, give it a quick whizz in the food processor to break up any large bits.

Bake the shortbread on the middle shelf of the oven for 12 minutes until pale golden. Leave to cool in the tin on a wire rack.

Place the dry ingredients for the crumble topping in a bowl and stir in the melted butter with your fingertips until the mixture starts to clump together.

Now for the cake. Cream the butter and sugar until really pale and light. Gradually add the beaten eggs, mixing well between each addition and scraping down the sides of the bowl with a rubber spatula from time to time. Add the lemon zest, vanilla and almond extract and mix again. Sift in the dry ingredients and beat until smooth, then add the soured cream and mix again.

Spread the jam evenly over the shortbread, leaving a 1cm border around the edge so it doesn't burn on the sides of the tin. Spoon over the cake mixture and spread level, arrange the cherries on top and scatter with the crumble. Bake on the middle shelf of the oven for 45 minutes–1 hour until golden brown, well risen and a skewer inserted into the middle comes out clean. Loosely cover the top with baking parchment if it appears to be browning too quickly.

Leave the cake to cool in the tin for 10 minutes, then run a palette knife around the edge to loosen the sides, remove from the tin and cool completely on a wire rack.

Chocolate, Cherry and Turrón Ice Cream

Turrón is almond nougat that hails from Spain, while torrone is the Italian version and can be found in hard (*duro*) or soft (*morbido*) varieties; for this recipe you'll need hard nougat. The cherry compote stirred though this rich chocolate ice cream is literally the cherry on the top – the combination of cherries, chocolate and almonds is the stuff of dreams.

SERVES 6–8

300ML FULL-FAT MILK

350ML DOUBLE CREAM

1 TABLESPOON COCOA POWDER

3 MEDIUM EGG YOLKS

200G GOLDEN CASTER SUGAR

1 TEASPOON VANILLA EXTRACT

A PINCH OF SALT

175G DARK CHOCOLATE, FINELY CHOPPED

For the cherry compote and nougat

400G RIPE DARK CHERRIES, WASHED

100G CASTER SUGAR

JUICE OF ½ LEMON

150G HARD ALMOND NOUGAT
(TURRÓN OR TORRONE)

WAFFLE CONES, TO SERVE

Equipment

ICE-CREAM MAKER

PLASTIC FREEZER BOX

Pour the milk and half the cream into a medium saucepan, add the cocoa and whisk to combine. Bring to the boil over a medium heat. Meanwhile, using a hand-held electric whisk, whisk together the egg yolks, sugar, vanilla and salt in a bowl until pale, smooth and light. Steadily pour over 3–4 tablespoons of the hot milk mixture and whisk constantly until smooth. Add the remaining milk mixture and whisk until combined. Return to the pan and cook over a low heat, stirring constantly, for about 3 minutes until the mixture thickens enough to coat the back of a spoon – don't let it boil or the eggs will scramble.

Tip the chopped chocolate into a bowl, pour the hot custard on top in a steady stream and whisk constantly until smooth and the chocolate has thoroughly melted. Add the remaining cream and whisk until silky smooth. Leave until cold and then cover and chill for at least 4 hours or overnight.

Meanwhile, prepare the cherry compote and nougat. Remove the stalk from each cherry and, holding it over a small saucepan to catch the juice, squeeze it between your fingers to pop out the stone. Very roughly chop the cherry flesh and add to the pan along with the sugar, lemon juice and 50ml cold water. Set over a low heat and stir constantly until the sugar has dissolved, then simmer gently for about 20 minutes until the cherries have softened and the juice is very thick and syrupy. Leave to cool. Cut the nougat into small dice.

Churn the chocolate custard in the ice-cream maker according to the manufacturer's instructions. Scoop into a plastic freezer box, add the cherry compote and nougat, mix to combine and freeze until firm.

Serve generous scoops of the ice cream in waffle cones.

Dried Cherry and Hazelnut Wafers for Cheese

These wafers are a cross between savoury biscotti and Melba toast, with a nod and a wink to soda bread along the way. I love dried sour cherries and am always looking for new ways to use them – normally they crop up in my sweet baking, but they pair especially well with nuts and creamy, almost grassy-tasting fresh goat's cheese.

MAKES ABOUT 30–40

UNSALTED BUTTER, FOR GREASING

100G WHOLE BLANCHED HAZELNUTS

75G DRIED SOUR CHERRIES

200G PLAIN FLOUR

150G WHOLEGRAIN SPELT FLOUR

½ TEASPOON BAKING POWDER

1 TEASPOON BICARBONATE OF SODA

A GOOD PINCH OF SEA SALT FLAKES

A GOOD GRINDING OF BLACK PEPPER

2 TABLESPOONS SOFT BROWN SUGAR

75G MIXED SEEDS, SUCH AS SUNFLOWER, PUMPKIN AND LINSEED

250ML BUTTERMILK

2 TABLESPOONS EXTRA VIRGIN OLIVE OIL

1 TABLESPOON CLEAR HONEY

Equipment

900G LOAF TIN

Preheat the oven to 170°C/gas mark 3. Grease and line the base and sides of the loaf tin with a strip of greased baking parchment.

Tip the hazelnuts onto a baking tray and toast in the oven for 4 minutes until pale golden. Leave to cool, then very roughly chop. Roughly chop the dried sour cherries if they are large.

Sift the flours, baking powder, bicarbonate of soda, salt and pepper into a large mixing bowl. Add the sugar, hazelnuts, dried cherries and seeds and mix to combine. In a jug, mix together the buttermilk, olive oil and honey. Add to the dry ingredients and mix well until combined, then use your hands to very lightly knead and bring the dough together until almost smooth.

Pat the dough into a rectangle slightly smaller than the tin and press into the tin to fill it right into the corners. Bake on the middle shelf of the oven for 35–40 minutes until risen, firm and golden. Leave to cool in the tin for 3–4 minutes and then turn out onto a wire rack until completely cold – about 4 hours. In the meantime, turn the oven off.

Preheat to the oven to 150°C/gas mark 2. Using a long, serrated bread knife, cut the loaf into slices no thicker than 2mm and arrange on baking parchment-covered trays. Bake in batches for 10–15 minutes on the middle shelf, swapping the trays around so that they cook evenly, until crisp and very lightly toasted.

Cool on wire racks before serving or storing in an airtight container until ready to eat – they will keep for up to 2 weeks.

Plum Ravioli

Feather-light pastries, filled with homemade plum compote, deep-fried and dusted heavily with icing sugar – I challenge you to eat just one! I have kept the sugar in the plum compote to a minimum, which makes it sharp and fruity and a nice contrast to the pastry and icing sugar, but if you have an especially sweet tooth you may want to increase it.

MAKES ABOUT 24

For the filling

500G RED OR PURPLE PLUMS, QUARTERED

75G CASTER SUGAR

FINELY GRATED ZEST AND JUICE OF ½ ORANGE

For the dough

300G PLAIN FLOUR, PLUS EXTRA FOR DUSTING

50G CASTER SUGAR

¼ TEASPOON BICARBONATE OF SODA

A GOOD PINCH OF GROUND CINNAMON

A PINCH OF SALT

FINELY GRATED ZEST OF ½ UNWAXED LEMON

4 TABLESPOONS MARSALA

55G UNSALTED BUTTER, MELTED AND SLIGHTLY COOLED

1 LARGE EGG, SEPARATED

1 LITRE SUNFLOWER OIL

ICING SUGAR, FOR DUSTING

Equipment

PASTA MACHINE

10–12CM PLAIN COOKIE CUTTER

SUGAR THERMOMETER

Start by making the filling. Place the plums, sugar and orange zest and juice in a saucepan and cook over a medium heat, stirring frequently, for about 30 minutes until the plums have cooked down to a jammy consistency. Keep a close eye on the mixture during the last moments of cooking and stir regularly to prevent it sticking and burning on the base of the pan. Tip into a bowl and leave to cool.

For the dough, sift the flour, caster sugar, bicarbonate of soda, cinnamon and salt into a mixing bowl. Make a well in the middle, and add the lemon zest, Marsala, melted butter and egg yolk. Mix well, adding a drop of water if needed to bring the dough together, but not too much, as it should be quite a dry dough. Knead for a couple of minutes until almost smooth. Cover with an upturned bowl or clingfilm and leave to rest for 20 minutes.

Set up the pasta machine at one end of a work surface and lightly dust with flour. Divide the dough into thirds – this makes it easier to work with. Roll one piece into a rectangle ½cm thick, keeping the remaining pieces covered. Pass through the pasta machine on the widest setting. Fold in half and pass through again, then repeat. Reduce the thickness of the rollers by one notch and pass the dough through again. Repeat, rolling at increasingly thinner increments, until the dough is 1mm thick – this is the last-but-one notch on my machine – keeping the work surface and your dough very lightly dusted with flour to prevent it sticking.

Lay the rolled-out dough across the work surface, being careful not to stretch it. Using the cutter, stamp out discs from the dough. Gather up the offcuts into a ball and set aside. Spoon slightly less than a teaspoonful of plum compote into the middle of each disc, leaving a ½cm border all round. Brush one side of the exposed dough with a little of the reserved, lightly beaten egg white, fold the dough over the compote to make a crescent shape and press the edges together to seal. Repeat with the remaining dough and compote. Any leftover dough can be thinly rolled, cut into strips, deep-fried and dusted with icing sugar.

Meanwhile, pour the oil into a large saucepan and set over a medium heat. Pop the thermometer into the pan and bring the oil up to 170–175°C.

Cook the ravioli in batches of around six in the hot oil for about 3 minutes until golden, ensuring that the oil returns to the correct temperature before cooking the next batch. Remove with a slotted spoon, drain well on kitchen paper and serve just warm, dusted with icing sugar.

Roasted Plum Soufflés

Soufflés strike fear into the heart of many cooks, but these little delights are very easy to make, requiring only a thick plum purée enriched with egg yolks and a mound of pillowy sweetened egg whites. They rise beautifully and are light yet fruity, making them perfect to serve at the end of a rich meal. The plum purée can be prepared in advance and the soufflés cooked just before serving.

MAKES 6

1 QUANTITY OF ROASTED PLUMS
(SEE PAGE 128)

1 TEASPOON CORNFLOUR

1 TEASPOON LEMON JUICE (OPTIONAL)

MELTED UNSALTED BUTTER, FOR GREASING

2 MEDIUM EGG YOLKS

4 MEDIUM EGG WHITES

A PINCH OF CREAM OF TARTAR

A PINCH OF SALT

75G CASTER SUGAR, PLUS EXTRA FOR DUSTING

THICK POURING CREAM, TO SERVE

Equipment
6 x 150ML RAMEKINS

Once the plums have roasted, leave them to cool, then scoop all the fruit and juice into a bowl, picking out and discarding the stones, vanilla pod pieces and cinnamon stick, and whizz until smooth using a stick blender or food processor. If you want a silky smooth sorbet pass through a fine-mesh nylon sieve. This should yield 475–500g purée. Place in a saucepan over a medium heat and cook gently, stirring frequently, for about 5 minutes until reduced to 400g. Mix the cornflour with a teaspoon of cold water, stir into the purée and simmer for another 30 seconds to thicken further and cook out the cornflour. Taste and add the lemon juice if it needs sharpening, remembering you will be adding sugar later. Leave to cool slightly.

Preheat the oven to 190°C/gas mark 5. Brush the inside of the ramekins neatly and smoothly with the melted butter, then dust with an even coating of caster sugar and tap out any excess. Spoon a rounded teaspoonful of plum purée into the base of each ramekin and spread level. Beat the egg yolks into the remaining plum purée.

In a large mixing bowl, whisk the egg whites with the cream of tartar and salt until they will hold soft, floppy peaks. Gradually add the caster sugar and whisk again until smooth and glossy.

Fold a large tablespoonful of the egg whites into the plum and egg yolk mixture to lighten it and then, using a large metal spoon, fold the purée back into the egg whites, being careful not to knock out the air. Spoon into the ramekins, slightly overfilling them and ensuring that the mixture fills them evenly without large air pockets. Using a palette knife, slice the excess mixture off the top of the soufflés level with the top of the ramekin. Run the tip of your thumb around the inside top edge of each ramekin and arrange on a solid baking tray.

Slide onto the middle shelf of the oven and bake for 10 minutes until well risen, golden brown on top and with a very slight wobble. Using a fish slice, carefully and quickly transfer the ramekins to small plates and serve immediately with thick pouring cream.

Crispy Duck with Spiced Plum Sauce

This plum sauce works perfectly as a dipping sauce for spring rolls and the like. The duck is also good with an Asian-style coleslaw and spring onion or chive pancakes. Make this the day before serving as the duck will need to marinate in the fridge overnight.

SERVES 4; MAKES 2 JARS

For the duck

1 ROUNDED TEASPOON SICHUAN PEPPERCORNS

2 GARLIC CLOVES, ROUGHLY CHOPPED

5CM PIECE OF FRESH GINGER, CHOPPED

1 ROUNDED TEASPOON CHINESE FIVE-SPICE

4 DUCK LEGS

2 TABLESPOONS SOY SAUCE

1 TABLESPOON CHINESE BLACK RICE VINEGAR

For the plum sauce

750G RED OR PURPLE PLUMS, ROUGHLY CHOPPED

1 SMALL RED ONION, CHOPPED

1 LARGE GARLIC CLOVE, CHOPPED

5CM PIECE OF FRESH GINGER, CHOPPED

1 RED CHILLI, DESEEDED AND CHOPPED

1 TEASPOON SICHUAN PEPPERCORNS

1 SMALL CINNAMON STICK

3 ALLSPICE BERRIES

1–2 STAR ANISE

125G SOFT LIGHT BROWN SUGAR

150ML CHINESE BLACK RICE VINEGAR

SOY SAUCE, TO TASTE (OPTIONAL)

SQUEEZE OF LIME JUICE, TO TASTE

To serve

PANCAKES

SHREDDED SPRING ONIONS AND CUCUMBER

Equipment

2 x 350G PRESERVING JARS

Start by preparing the duck. Tip the Sichuan peppercorns into a small dry frying pan and toast over a low–medium heat for a couple of minutes until they begin to smell aromatic. Grind using a pestle and mortar. Add the garlic and ginger to the mortar along with the five-spice and pound until almost smooth.

Lay the duck legs on a large platter and slash the skin on each leg a couple of times. Drizzle with the soy sauce and vinegar, rubbing it into both the meat and skin side of each leg. Using your hands, massage the spice mix into each leg to coat as evenly as possible. Cover with clingfilm and chill in the fridge overnight.

To make the plum sauce, place the plums, onion, garlic, ginger and chilli in a large stainless steel saucepan. Pop the spices into the pan, add the sugar and vinegar and mix to combine. Place the pan over a low–medium heat and bring to the boil, stirring frequently to dissolve the sugar. Cook steadily for about 40 minutes, stirring from time to time, until the fruit is very tender and the mixture thickened.

Either push the mixture through a fine-mesh nylon sieve or a moulin à légumes to remove the spices and plum skins. Quickly wash the pan, return the strained sauce to it and cook for a further 3–4 minutes until thickened to the consistency of tomato ketchup. Taste the sauce and add a dash of soy sauce if it needs saltiness and a drop of freshly squeezed lime juice to sharpen it.

Spoon into a jar or bowl and leave until cold, then spoon into a sterilised Kilner or other preserving jar (see page 132), seal and store in the fridge until needed. It will keep well for up to 6 weeks.

The next day, preheat the oven to 190°C/gas mark 5. Pat the duck legs dry, rubbing off as much of the marinade as possible, arrange in a roasting tin and cook in the oven for 25–30 minutes until the skin is crisp and the meat tender.

Shred the duck and serve Peking style with the plum sauce, along with pancakes and shredded spring onions and cucumber.

Roasted Plums with Rice Pudding

Plums are enormously versatile and roasting them in this super-simple fashion will expand their uses even further. Although divine dished up just as they are or with a good puddle of cream, they are sublime served alongside rice pudding, as here, or when turned into a sorbet, soufflé or unctuous cheesecake. Try them with your breakfast yogurt and granola or with a hot bowl of porridge – the list goes on…

I always recommend that you use ripe fruit for most recipes, but roasting slightly under-ripe plums will enhance any that are slightly lacking in the flavour department.

SERVES 6

For the roasted plums

800G RIPE RED PLUMS, WASHED

1½ TABLESPOONS CASTER SUGAR

½ VANILLA POD

1 SMALL CINNAMON STICK

For the rice pudding

125G PUDDING OR SHORT-GRAIN RICE

50–75G CASTER SUGAR

1 VANILLA POD, SPLIT IN HALF LENGTHWAYS

1 STRIP OF ORANGE PEEL

2 GREEN CARDAMOM PODS, LIGHTLY CRUSHED

750ML SEMI-SKIMMED MILK

A PINCH OF SALT

2–3 TABLESPOONS DOUBLE CREAM, PLUS EXTRA TO SERVE

1 TABLESPOON CHOPPED PISTACHIOS, ALMONDS OR HAZELNUTS

Preheat the oven to 180°C/gas mark 4 and line a baking tin with baking parchment or foil.

For the roasted plums, cut the fruits in half – don't worry about removing the stones at this stage. Arrange in the lined tin, cut-side uppermost, and sprinkle with the sugar. Split the half vanilla pod in half down its length and cut each piece in half again. Tuck the vanilla pieces and cinnamon stick amongst the plums and roast on the middle shelf of the oven for 30–40 minutes until the fruit is very tender, juicy and starting to caramelise at the edges.

Meanwhile, make the rice pudding. Place the rice in a saucepan, add 350ml cold water and bring to the boil. Reduce the heat and simmer for 4–5 minutes. Drain and return to the pan.

Add the vanilla pod to the rice with 50g sugar, the strip of orange peel, cardamom pods, milk and salt. Place over a low heat and bring slowly to the boil. Simmer very gently, stirring from time to time, for about 20 minutes until the rice is tender and most of the milk has been absorbed.

Remove from the heat, fish out the vanilla pod and orange peel and add the cream and the rest of the sugar, if needed. Serve warm, scattered with the nuts, with the roasted plums and extra cream.

Roasted Plum Sorbet

My sister and I meet for a 'light' supper in Soho about once a month and the evening generally follows the same pattern each time. We aim to eat somewhere vaguely healthy – as we're more often than not pretending to be watching what we eat – and then we amble through the streets of Central London to our favourite gelato bar and undo all the good we did earlier. This recipe is inspired by a sorbet that I had on one such evening in late summer, the scoops piled high into a waffle cone and dripping sticky-sweet plum juices down my hands – the perfect end to an evening.

SERVES 6–8

1 QUANTITY OF ROASTED PLUMS
(SEE PAGE 128)

150G CASTER SUGAR

Equipment

ICE-CREAM MAKER

Once the plums have roasted, leave them to cool, then scoop all the fruit and juice into a bowl, picking out and discarding the stones, vanilla pod pieces and cinnamon stick as you do so. Whizz the plums until smooth – I find this easiest using a stick blender, but otherwise transfer to a food processor – and then pass through a fine-mesh nylon sieve if you want a silky smooth sorbet. I don't mind the odd speckle of plum skin in the sorbet but it's down to personal preference.

Pour 200ml cold water into a saucepan and add the caster sugar. Bring to the boil over a medium heat, stirring to dissolve the sugar. Simmer for 2 minutes, then remove from the heat and add the roasted plum purée. Leave to cool, then cover and chill in the fridge for a couple of hours before churning in the ice-cream maker according to the manufacturer's instructions.

An ice-cream maker will make a lighter sorbet, but if you
don't have one, simply freeze the mixture in a plastic freezer
box, whisking it every couple of hours to break up the ice crystals.
Once the sorbet has frozen, break it into manageable chunks, tip
into a food processor and blend until smooth and light. Return
to the freezer box and freeze until firm.

Plum and Star Anise Jam

I like jam to be soft-set – I don't want to be able to stand my spoon up in the jar, but for the jam to dribble off my toast and onto my fingers so that I get in a sticky, fruity mess and have to add more. With that in mind, I err on the side of less sugar to fruit, which allows the fruitiness to shine through, though it does require perfectly ripe, juicy fruit.

MAKES 4–5 JARS

1.5KG RIPE PLUMS, WASHED

800G GRANULATED OR JAM SUGAR

1 CINNAMON STICK

2 STAR ANISE

Equipment

4–5 x 450G JAM JARS

STAINLESS STEEL PRESERVING PAN

JAM FUNNEL (OPTIONAL)

Cut the plums into quarters, remove the stones and tip into a large glass or ceramic bowl. Add the sugar and stir well to thoroughly combine. Add the cinnamon stick and star anise and stir again. Cover with clingfilm and leave at room temperature for 6–8 hours or overnight to allow the sugar to start to dissolve in the fruit juices.

Scoop the contents of the bowl into the preserving pan and set over a low heat to dissolve any remaining sugar. Increase the heat to medium and bring to the boil, removing any scum that rises to the surface with a slotted spoon. Cook for about 20 minutes at a steady boil until the jam just reaches setting point. To test for setting point, drop a scant teaspoon of jam onto a chilled saucer, leave it for 30 seconds and then push it with the tip of your finger. If the jam forms a light skin and wrinkles, it's ready; if not, continue to cook and test every couple of minutes until setting point has been reached.

Once setting point has been reached, remove the pan from the heat and leave to relax for 5 minutes – this will allow any larger fruit pieces to remain suspended in the jam once it is bottled rather than rising to the top of the jar.

Pick out the cinnamon stick and star anise, ladle the jam into a jug and pour into the warm sterilised jars – using a jam funnel will make this an easier task. Using a clean, damp cloth, wipe the edges of the jars to remove any drips and screw the lids on tightly. Leave until completely cold before labelling and storing in a cool, dark cupboard for up to 6 months and up to 2 months in the fridge after opening.

To sterilise jam jars, preheat the oven to 120°C/gas mark ½. Wash the jam jars and their lids in hot soapy water, dry and place just the jars on a baking tray in the oven to sterilise for at least 10 minutes while the jam is boiling. Do not heat the lids as they can melt in the oven. Pop two saucers into the fridge or freezer ready for testing the jam for setting point.

White Peach and Raspberry Jam

Peaches and raspberries are a wonderful combination, particularly in this jam. Although raspberry jam is delicious, it can be heavy on the seeds, so my solution is to combine the berries with other fruits. If you can find white peaches, do use them here – the colour is quite divine. You could also add the seeds scraped from a split vanilla pod if you like.

MAKES 4–5 JARS

750G OR 4–5 LARGE WHITE-FLESHED PEACHES, WASHED

650G GRANULATED OR JAM SUGAR

JUICE OF 1 LEMON

350G RASPBERRIES

Equipment

4–5 x 450G JAM JARS

STAINLESS STEEL PRESERVING PAN

JAM FUNNEL (OPTIONAL)

Cut the peaches into wedges, removing the stones as you do so. Tip the wedges into a large glass or ceramic bowl and add the sugar and lemon juice, stirring well to thoroughly combine. Cover with clingfilm and leave at room temperature for 4 hours to allow the sugar to start to dissolve in the juices released from the peaches.

Sterilise the jam jars and chill two saucers to test for setting point, as for the Plum and Star Anise Jam (opposite). Scoop the sugary peaches into the preserving pan, add the raspberries and then follow the method for the plum jam opposite from the second step to finish making the jam.

Apricot and Vanilla Jam

This jam in particular makes my case for majoring on fruitiness rather than sweetness. Adding the kernels from the apricot stones contributes a nutty, almondy note to the end result.

MAKES 4–5 JARS

1.2KG RIPE APRICOTS, WASHED

750G GRANULATED OR JAM SUGAR

JUICE OF 1 LEMON

1 VANILLA POD, SPLIT IN HALF LENGTHWAYS

Equipment

4–5 x 450G JAM JARS

STAINLESS STEEL PRESERVING PAN

JAM FUNNEL (OPTIONAL)

Cut the apricots into quarters, reserving the stones. Tip into a large glass bowl and add the sugar and lemon juice. Mix well, cover and leave at room temperature for 6–8 hours or overnight to allow the sugar to start to draw out and dissolve in the fruit juices. Meanwhile, take one apricot stone at a time, wrap in a clean tea towel and bash with a rolling pin to crack the shell. Remove the kernel and set aside.

Sterilise the jam jars and chill two saucers to test for setting point, as for the Plum and Star Anise Jam, opposite. Bring a small saucepan of water to the boil, add the apricot kernels and blanch for 1–2 minutes, then drain and set aside.

Scoop the contents of the bowl into the preserving pan, add the vanilla pod and follow the method for the plum jam opposite from the second step to finish making the jam. When bottling, ensure that the apricot kernels are evenly divided between the jars.

Plum Streuselkuchen

This enriched dough has more in common with a cake than bread and is ideal to serve for a late breakfast, brunch or mid-morning treat with a pot of steaming coffee. It's best eaten on the day of making but will reheat well if wrapped in foil and placed in a moderate oven for a few minutes. You can prepare the dough the night before and leave it to prove in the fridge overnight before topping and baking. I like to use a mixture of plums for this cake, not only for flavour but for colour too.

SERVES 8–10

100ML FULL-FAT MILK

300G PLAIN FLOUR

125G CASTER SUGAR

½ TEASPOON GROUND CINNAMON

7G FAST-ACTION/EASY-BLEND DRIED YEAST

A GOOD PINCH OF SALT

75G SOURED CREAM, BUTTERMILK AT ROOM TEMPERATURE

1 MEDIUM EGG

1 MEDIUM EGG YOLK

1 TEASPOON FINELY GRATED UNWAXED LEMON ZEST

1 TEASPOON VANILLA EXTRACT

125G UNSALTED BUTTER, DICED AND SOFTENED, PLUS EXTRA FOR GREASING

500G MIXED PLUMS, WASHED AND DRIED

For the streusel

50G SOFT LIGHT BROWN SUGAR

50G SOFT DARK BROWN SUGAR

A GOOD PINCH OF SALT

½ TEASPOON GROUND CINNAMON

85G PLAIN FLOUR

60G UNSALTED BUTTER, MELTED

Equipment

20CM SQUARE CAKE TIN

Grease the tin and line the base and sides with greased baking parchment.

Warm the milk until tepid – a shade hotter than body temperature. Tip the flour into the bowl of a free-standing mixer fitted with a dough hook. Add the caster sugar, cinnamon, yeast and salt and mix with a balloon whisk to thoroughly combine. Make a well in the middle. Combine the soured cream or buttermilk, whole egg, yolk, lemon zest and vanilla extract in a jug. Tip the warm milk into the bowl, add the soured cream mixture and softened butter and knead on a medium speed for about 4 minutes until you have a silky smooth dough.

Scoop into the prepared tin and spread level using a palette knife. Cover loosely with clingfilm and either leave the dough to prove slowly overnight in the fridge or for 2–3 hours at room temperature.

If you have proved the dough overnight in the fridge, bring it to room temperature before proceeding to the next stage. Preheat the oven to 190°C/gas mark 5.

Meanwhile, prepare the streusel. Mix the sugars, salt, cinnamon and flour in a small bowl. Add the melted butter and stir well to combine – the mixture should start to form large clumps. Scatter one-third over the top of the cake. Cut the plums into quarters or sixths, depending on size, and arrange on top. Scatter the remaining streusel over the plums.

Bake the streuselkuchen on the middle shelf of the oven for 20 minutes. Reduce the heat to 170°C/gas mark 3 and bake for a further 45–50 minutes until the cake is well risen, the streusel golden and crisp, the fruit tender and a wooden skewer inserted into the middle of the cake comes out clean.

Damson Pâté de Fruit

Damsons – small, dark blue plums – are too bitter to be eaten raw but have a unique flavour once cooked and shown a little sugar. I like them just like that or tossed into a pie or crumble followed by the inevitable game of Tinker, Tailor, Soldier, Sailor. But they have a relatively short season, so are worth cooking with in as many ways as you can, and this is a valuable recipe to add to the repertoire. I love making *pâte de fruit* and am always looking for new fruits to give the pastille treatment to. The purée can be prepared and frozen in batches until ready to use, if you are like me and can't bear to be without your favourite fruits once the season is over.

MAKES ABOUT 40 PIECES

SUNFLOWER OIL, FOR OILING

600G DAMSONS, WASHED

1–2 TABLESPOONS LEMON JUICE

400G CASTER SUGAR

12G POWDERED PECTIN (TATE & LYLE BRAND)

150G GRANULATED SUGAR, FOR COATING

Equipment

20CM SQUARE BAKING TIN

Lightly oil the baking tin and line the base and sides with clingfilm, ensuring that it comes right up the sides of the tin.

Tip the damsons into a saucepan that will accommodate them spaciously. Add the lemon juice and 2–3 tablespoons of the caster sugar, cover and cook over a low heat, stirring from time to time, for about 20 minutes until the fruit has burst and become really soft and juicy. Tip into a fine-mesh nylon sieve set over a bowl and push the fruit through until all that remains in the sieve is a little damson skin and the stones. Return the purée to the cleaned pan and reheat until boiling, then simmer for 2 minutes to thicken slightly.

In a bowl, whisk together the remaining caster sugar and pectin – it needs to be thoroughly combined before adding to the purée. Add to the pan, stirring constantly with a wooden spoon or heatproof rubber spatula to dissolve the sugar. Simmer over a medium heat, stirring frequently, until the mixture has thickened and a teaspoonful dropped into a small bowl of iced water immediately forms into a ball. Continue cooking and testing every couple of minutes until setting point has been reached.

Pour into the prepared tin and spread level. Leave in a cool place until completely cold and then cover with clingfilm and leave until firm – preferably overnight.

The next day, tip the granulated sugar onto a baking tray in an even layer. Carefully turn out the *pâte de fruit* onto the sugar, top-side down. Peel off the clingfilm from the underside and, using a hot or lightly greased kitchen knife, cut into 1.5–2cm squares, coating each piece in the sugar as you do so to prevent them sticking together.

Leave the pastilles to dry for 30 minutes–1 hour before shaking off the excess sugar and packaging into pretty boxes between layers of waxed or non-stick paper.

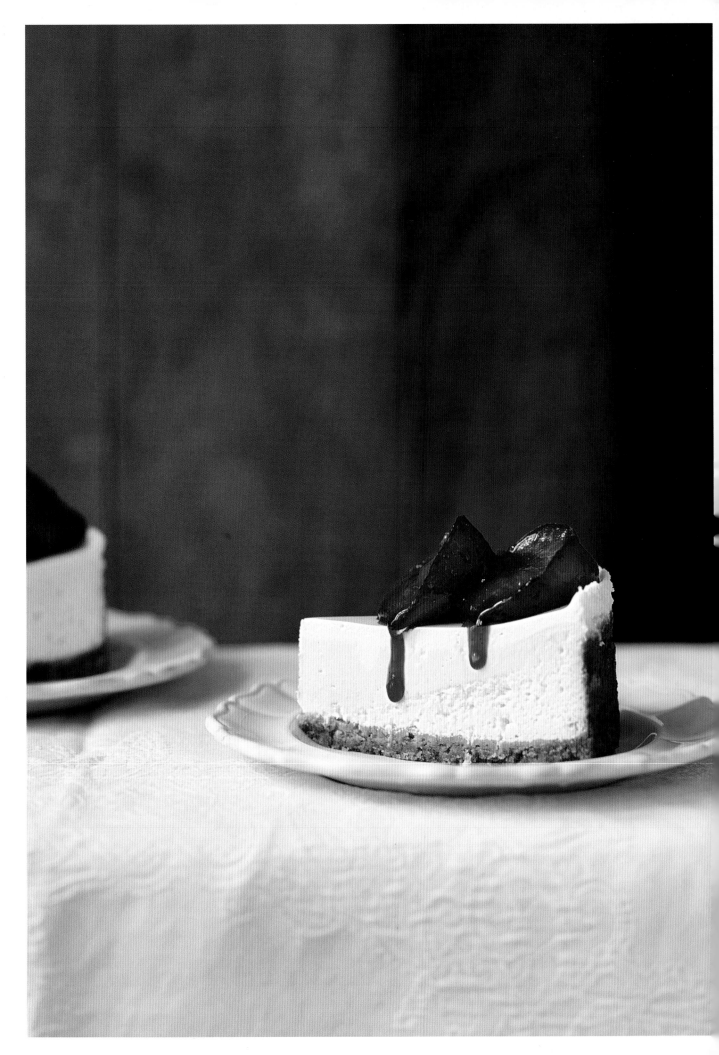

New York-style Cheesecake with Roasted Plums

This cheesecake is best made the day before serving, giving it plenty of time to cool, which will make slicing easier. The Roasted Plums are the perfect accompaniment, being fruity and sharp enough to cut through the creamy richness.

SERVES 8

150G DIGESTIVE BISCUITS, GINGERSNAPS OR AMARETTI

50G UNSALTED BUTTER, MELTED, PLUS EXTRA FOR GREASING

600G FULL-FAT CREAM CHEESE

3 LARGE EGGS

300ML SOURED CREAM

150G CASTER SUGAR

1 TABLESPOON CORNFLOUR

1 TEASPOON VANILLA EXTRACT

GRATED ZEST AND JUICE OF 1 UNWAXED LEMON

100G GREEK STYLE YOGURT

ROASTED PLUMS (SEE PAGE 128), TO SERVE

Equipment
20CM SPRINGFORM CAKE TIN

Preheat the oven to 170°C/gas mark 3. Grease the tin and line the base with a disc of greased baking parchment.

Finely crush the biscuits, either in a food processor or in a freezer bag using a rolling pin, and tip into a bowl. Mix in the melted butter. Tip into the prepared tin and press into an even layer over the base. Bake on the middle shelf of the oven for 5 minutes.

Meanwhile, place the cream cheese, eggs, half the soured cream, 100g of the caster sugar and the cornflour in a food processor and whizz until smooth. Scrape down the sides of the bowl with a rubber spatula and then add the vanilla extract and lemon zest and juice and whizz again.

Remove the tin from the oven and carefully pour the mixture over the biscuit base. Place on a solid baking tray and bake on the middle shelf of the oven for about 35 minutes or until just set. Remove from the oven and leave the cheesecake to rest for 10 minutes, leaving the oven on.

Beat together the remaining soured cream, the yogurt and remaining 50g of caster sugar. Carefully spoon this mixture on top of the cheesecake and return to the oven for a further 10 minutes until set but not coloured. Leave the cheesecake to cool completely before chilling.

Serve the cheesecake in slices with the Roasted Plums and their syrupy juices.

Vanilla and Thyme Baked Apricots

The fresh apricot season seems to come and go in a flash, so make the most of them while they're around. More often than not the ones you see in the shops are under-ripe and disappointing when eaten raw. They fare much better when shown a little heat, a little love and something sweet to bring out their flavour and juiciness. This is the simplest and most delicious way of doing so, and even less-than-impressive apricots come alive when baked. Serve warm rather than hot, with the juices poured over and with a good slug of thick double cream. Or save for breakfast and top with natural yogurt and granola – preferably homemade, of course. It's one of those recipes where you don't need to be too specific – add a little more honey if you prefer and maybe a cinnamon stick, or even a handful of lightly toasted flaked almonds or pine nuts for crunch.

SERVES 3–4

10–12 RIPE APRICOTS

4 STRIPS OF UNWAXED LEMON PEEL

JUICE OF ½ LEMON

1 VANILLA POD

3 SPRIGS OF THYME

2–3 TABLESPOONS CLEAR HONEY

CHILLED DOUBLE CREAM, TO SERVE

Preheat the oven to 190°C/gas mark 5.

Wash the apricots and pat dry. Cut in half, remove the stones and arrange the fruit, cut-side uppermost, in a single layer in a ceramic ovenproof dish. Tuck the strips of lemon peel in amongst the fruit and drizzle over the lemon juice. Using the point of a knife, slice the vanilla pod in half down its length and nestle both halves and the thyme sprigs around the apricots. Finally, drizzle over the honey and 2 tablespoons of cold water.

Bake on the middle shelf of the oven for 20–25 minutes until tender, basting the apricots with the resulting juices halfway through cooking. The cooking timings can vary depending on the size and ripeness of the apricots, so keep an eye on them after 20 minutes, as you want the fruit to still hold its shape without becoming overly soft and mushy.

Serve warm with cold double cream.

Apricot and Vanilla Tart

Apricots nestled in a rich custard and baked inside a crisp, almondy pastry – this is high summer in a tart and perfect for a lunch or dinner in the garden. When the fruits are not in peak condition, I suggest cooking with them to bring out their good side and this tart is sure to do just that. It's best served on the day of making, perhaps decorated with fresh lavender, and with extra crème fraîche, or vanilla ice cream if you're feeling indulgent – not that it needs it of course!

SERVES 8

For the pastry

150G PLAIN FLOUR, PLUS EXTRA FOR DUSTING

75G GROUND ALMONDS

50G CASTER SUGAR

125G UNSALTED BUTTER, CHILLED AND DICED

A GOOD PINCH OF SEA SALT

½ TABLESPOON ICED WATER

1 TEASPOON LEMON JUICE OR CIDER VINEGAR

1 MEDIUM EGG YOLK, LIGHTLY BEATEN

For the filling

750G–1KG APRICOTS, WASHED, DRIED, HALVED AND STONED

1 VANILLA POD OR 1 TEASPOON VANILLA BEAN PASTE

250ML CRÈME FRAÎCHE

1 MEDIUM EGG

2 MEDIUM EGG YOLKS

115G CASTER SUGAR

50G FLAKED ALMONDS

ICING SUGAR, TO DECORATE

Equipment

22CM FLUTED TART TIN, 4CM DEEP

Start by making the pastry. In a food processor, pulse together the flour, ground almonds, sugar, butter and salt until there are only a very few small streaks of butter visible. Tip into a bowl and make a well in the centre. Mix the water with the lemon juice or vinegar and add to the bowl with the egg yolk. Bring the dough together using a palette knife and then, using your hands, gather the dough into a ball, being careful not to overwork it. Flatten into a disc, wrap in clingfilm and chill for a good couple of hours until firm.

Dust the work surface with flour and roll out the pastry into a disc at least 4cm larger all round than the tart tin. Carefully roll the pastry up around the rolling pin and unroll into the tin, ensuring that it is centrally positioned. Press the dough into the corners and flutes of the tin and trim off any excess from the top using a sharp knife. Prick the base with a fork and chill for 20 minutes while you prepare the filling and preheat the oven to 190°C/gas mark 5. Place a solid baking tray on the middle shelf of the oven.

Arrange the apricot halves cut-side uppermost in tight concentric circles, each slightly overlapping, in the pastry case. If using, split the vanilla pod in half down its length with a small sharp knife and scrape the seeds into a bowl, or add the vanilla bean paste. Add the crème fraîche, whole egg, yolks and caster sugar and whisk until smooth. Slowly pour the custard around the apricots, scatter with the flaked almonds and slide the tart onto the hot baking tray. Bake for about 1 hour until the pastry is golden brown, the custard puffed and set and the apricots starting to brown at the edges. You may need to turn the tart around halfway through to ensure that it cooks evenly.

Leave to cool to room temperature and serve with a light dusting of icing sugar.

Peach and Buffalo Mozzarella Salad with Pistachio Pesto

I have rather romantic notions of making this salad after a leisurely stroll around an Italian market, carefully selecting the ripest peaches, most peppery rocket and most beautiful tomatoes. As with all simple salads, success lies in using the absolute best, most flavoursome produce you can find, so save this for high summer when the peaches are juicy and the tomatoes have been warmed by the sun. Failing that, get yourself to Italy and join me for a market wander. You can make it with burrata if you prefer, but it can be a little too creamy for my taste.

SERVES 4

4 RIPE PEACHES, WASHED AND DRIED

1 LEBANESE CUCUMBER OR ½ REGULAR CUCUMBER

6 HEIRLOOM TOMATOES, PREFERABLY MIXED COLOURS

A GOOD HANDFUL OF WILD ROCKET

2 x 125G BALLS BUFFALO MOZZARELLA

A HANDFUL OF PURPLE BASIL

3 TABLESPOONS AGED BALSAMIC VINEGAR

3 TABLESPOONS EXTRA VIRGIN OLIVE OIL

FRESHLY GROUND BLACK PEPPER

For the pistachio pesto

50G SHELLED UNSALTED PISTACHIOS, LIGHTLY TOASTED

1 GARLIC CLOVE, PEELED

30G FLAT-LEAF PARSLEY

A DASH OF LEMON JUICE

100ML EXTRA VIRGIN OR PISTACHIO OIL

SALT AND FRESHLY GROUND BLACK PEPPER

First make the pesto. Tip the lightly toasted pistachios into the bowl of a mini processor and whizz until finely chopped. Add the garlic and parsley and whizz again to combine. Then add the lemon juice and half of the oil, season well with salt and black pepper and blend until almost smooth. Add the remaining oil and whizz once more. Set aside for 30 minutes for all of the flavours to mingle, after which time taste the pesto and add more salt and pepper as needed.

Cut the peaches in half, remove the stones and cut the fruit into wedges. Cut the cucumber into bite-sized pieces and slice the tomatoes. Arrange the rocket on each plate and top with peaches, cucumber and tomatoes. Tear the mozzarella into pieces and divide between the plates. Spoon the pesto over each salad and scatter with the basil. Finish with a drizzle of the balsamic vinegar and extra virgin olive oil and a good grinding of black pepper.

Peach Shrub

Shrub is the name given to either a vinegared fruit syrup or to alcohol, often rum or brandy, that has fruit steeped in it. For this recipe we're sticking with the former . Don't turn the page yet, though, dismissing the notion of vinegared fruit syrup as the ramblings of a mad woman. When I was playing around with this recipe, most people I asked to taste test for me were sceptical at first. But what they discovered was a remarkably clean-tasting cordial – the vinegar is there but as an acidic back note to the vibrant peachy syrup.

Vinegar shrubs date from colonial America and were traditionally a way of preserving soft fruits, the vinegar acting as a preservative. They fell out of favour when commercially made cordials became widely available and with the advent of home refrigeration. Shrubs are now experiencing something of a renaissance and are deliciously refreshing when diluted with soda water and served with a good handful of ice or added to cocktails – try mixing with a measure of good-quality bourbon, vodka or gin, topped up with dry ginger, tonic water or soda water.

MAKES 1 LARGE BOTTLE

6 RIPE YELLOW-FLESHED PEACHES, WASHED

350G CASTER SUGAR

300ML WHITE BALSAMIC VINEGAR

Equipment

LARGE KILNER OR OTHER PRESERVING JAR

FINE-MESH NYLON SIEVE

PIECE OF CLEAN MUSLIN

500ML BOTTLE WITH CAP

Cut the peaches in half and remove the stones. Slice the fruit directly into a ceramic mixing bowl or large Kilner or other preserving jar. Add the sugar and mix to combine. Cover and pop in the fridge for 2 days, stirring twice a day until the fruit is super-soft and very juicy. You'll be amazed at how much juice is released from the fruit.

Add the vinegar, stir well, cover and return to the fridge for another day, again stirring twice a day.

Tip the whole thing through a fine-mesh nylon sieve into a bowl and leave for a couple of hours to ensure that every last drop of juice drips through into the bowl. Don't be tempted to push the fruit, otherwise you'll end up with a cloudy pulp rather than clear syrup. Finally, pass the resulting liquid through clean muslin before decanting into a sterilised bottle (see page 132). The shrub will keep for up to 1 month in the fridge.

When making shrub, it is of the utmost importance that you use ripe fruit, as you need to extract maximum flavour from the fruit and anything under-ripe won't have the necessary oomph and juice. If I happen to have a mixture of peaches in the fruit bowl – flat, white or yellow-fleshed – I toss them all in together, sometimes adding a handful of raspberries or a couple of slices of fresh ginger for extra zing. The type of vinegar used plays an important part here too. I tried variations with cider vinegar and good-quality white wine vinegar but discovered that I much prefer using white balsamic. It has a more rounded, less acidic, less vinegary hit and is now widely available in larger supermarkets or in good delis.

Peach and Caramelised Honey Zabaglione Ice Cream with Pistachio Tuiles

Zabaglione is one of my all-time favourite desserts, whether served over sugared and sliced strawberries or peaches – the combination of eggs, sugar and Marsala whisked over heat to produce pale clouds of deliciousness is quite dreamy. I also like zabaglione cooled and folded into softly whipped cream. And I like ice cream and peaches. So I've put all of those things together here. For the purists out there, I am aware that this is not strictly zabaglione, but this ice cream does at least have all the necessary elements – with a few added extras. The honey gives the ice cream a slightly softer set while enhancing the peachiness of the fruit. For best results, your peaches must be ripe and juicy – not only will under-ripe fruit be tricky to skin but the flavour will be somewhat less fabulous. As the ice cream recipe uses only egg yolks, I've included a recipe for Pistachio Tuiles that will at least go some way to using up the egg whites and provide you with something biscuity to serve with the ice cream. They are best eaten on the day of making, but can be kept in an airtight container for a further day and crisped up in a moderate oven.

SERVES 6

For the ice cream

4 LARGE, RIPE YELLOW-FLESHED PEACHES

125G CLEAR FRAGRANT HONEY

JUICE OF ½ LEMON

175ML FULL-FAT MILK

300ML DOUBLE CREAM

½ VANILLA POD, SPLIT IN HALF LENGTHWAYS

4 MEDIUM EGG YOLKS

75G CASTER SUGAR

2–3 TABLESPOONS MARSALA

A SMALL PINCH OF SALT

For the pistachio tuiles

50G SHELLED UNSALTED PISTACHIOS

125G CASTER SUGAR

60G PLAIN FLOUR

3 MEDIUM EGG WHITES

A PINCH OF SALT

½ TEASPOON VANILLA EXTRACT

75G UNSALTED BUTTER, MELTED AND SLIGHTLY COOLED

Equipment

ICE-CREAM MAKER

PLASTIC FREEZER BOX

Cut a small cross on the underside of each peach. Place in a bowl, cover with boiling water and leave for 30 seconds. Drain and run cold water over to loosen the skins; they should now slip off easily with the aid of the knife. Cut the peaches into quarters, discarding the stones, and slice into wedges.

Bring the honey to the boil in a medium saucepan over a low–medium heat, then cook gently until reduced by nearly half and starting to darken to an amber-coloured caramel. Add the peaches and lemon juice, combine, and cook, stirring frequently for 8–10 minutes until the peaches break down into a pulp. Using a stick blender or food processor, blend the mixture until smooth.

Pour the milk and half the cream into a medium, heavy-bottomed pan. Add the split vanilla pod, bring slowly to the boil and then immediately remove from the heat and leave to infuse for 10 minutes.

Using a hand-held electric whisk, whisk the egg yolks with the sugar in a bowl until really pale and light. Add the Marsala and salt and whisk to combine. Reheat the milk, then pour onto the egg yolk mixture and whisk constantly until smooth. Return to the pan and heat gently, stirring constantly, until thick enough to coat the back of a wooden spoon – don't allow it boil or you might scramble the eggs.

Remove from the heat, add the remaining cream and the peach purée and whisk to combine. Strain into a clean bowl and leave until completely cold. Cover and chill for at least 2 hours but preferably overnight, then churn in the ice-cream maker according to the manufacturer's instructions. Scoop into a plastic freezer box and freeze until needed.

For the tuiles, finely chop the pistachios in a food processor – you still want visible nutty pieces. Add the sugar and flour and whizz again until combined.

Whisk the egg whites with the salt in a bowl until they hold soft, floppy peaks. Add the vanilla and whisk to combine. Fold in the dry ingredients using a large metal spoon. Pour the melted butter around the sides of the bowl and fold in until thoroughly combined. Cover with clingfilm and chill for 1 hour.

Preheat the oven to 150°C/gas mark 2 and line 2 baking trays with baking parchment. Drop 4 dessertspoonfuls of mixture onto each tray and spread each into thin 10–12cm discs. Bake on the middle shelf for 10–12 minutes until starting to turn golden brown at the edges. Working quickly, slide a palette knife under each tuile, lift off the tray and either wrap around a wooden spoon handle or drape over a rolling pin. They will harden very quickly, which is why you bake only a few at a time. Repeat until all the batter has been used up.

Poached Peaches with Vanilla and Lemon Verbena

You can use either white- or yellow-fleshed peaches for this recipe, but I do love the rather elegant subtle hues of the white variety. Add a handful of fresh raspberries or redcurrants to the peaches after poaching for a pop of colour and contrast.

SERVES 6

100G CASTER SUGAR

2 STRIPS OF PEEL FROM AN UNWAXED LEMON

2 STRIPS OF ORANGE PEEL

JUICE OF ½ LEMON

450ML SWEET WINE, SUCH AS MUSCAT OR LILLET ROSÉ

1 VANILLA POD, SPLIT IN HALF LENGTHWAYS

1 LARGE SPRIG OF LEMON VERBENA

6 RIPE PEACHES

A HANDFUL OF RASPBERRIES OR REDCURRANTS (OPTIONAL)

To make the poaching syrup, place the sugar, lemon and orange peels, lemon juice and sweet wine into a deep sauté pan. Add the vanilla pod with the lemon verbena and 450ml cold water. Bring slowly to the boil to dissolve the sugar, then lower the heat to a very gentle simmer.

Meanwhile, prepare the peaches. Cut a small cross through the skin on the underside of each peach. Place in a large bowl, cover with boiling water and leave for 30 seconds–1 minute to loosen the skin, then drain and rinse under cold water. Carefully peel the peaches.

Gently lower the peaches into the simmering syrup, cover with a disc of baking parchment and poach for about 15 minutes or until tender when tested with the point of a small, sharp knife – the cooking time will vary depending on the ripeness of the fruit.

Using a slotted spoon, transfer the peaches to a bowl. Increase the heat under the poaching syrup and boil until reduced by one-third of its original volume. Strain and pour over the peaches, add a handful of raspberries or redcurrants if you like and leave until cold.

Tropical

It was really tempting to throw the doors open wide with tropical fruit and include such delights as tamarillos and guavas, but instead I have attempted to stick to those fruits that are more readily available year round.

Most tropical fruits, with the exception of persimmons and melons, come from the southern hemisphere, as they require warmer climes and degrees of humidity. Persimmons also grow well in California, among other places, and melons in the more southern European countries.

Almost all tropical fruits protect their sweet delicate flesh with a thick and sometimes impenetrable skin – think coconuts and pineapples. This can make testing for ripeness tricky. When buying melons I always smell the underside of the fruit – it should smell sweet, aromatic and 'melony' if ripe and ready to eat. Probably the only time that I'll suggest using under-ripe fruit in a recipe is when making green papaya salad – a classic dish served throughout South East Asia in one guise or another. Green papayas are large under-ripe fruits often sold in the veg section of Asian supermarkets.

If you've ever travelled to the tropics then you have no doubt eaten fragrant, aromatic mangoes, bananas and papayas – the like of which we rarely get to see in northern Europe – as fruit is picked at its peak of ripeness and intended to be eaten fresh rather than being packed into crates and shipped around the world. India is one of the largest producers of mangoes in the world but only a very small percentage is exported. Luckily for us, fabulous mangoes are also grown from Brazil to Thailand. They vary hugely in size, colour and sweetness, with some of the best varieties having a bright egg-yolk yellow, silky smooth, almost buttery flesh.

Green Papaya Salad with Crispy Fried Beef

Green papayas, or pawpaws, are large, under-ripe papayas that are used as a vegetable in Thai or Vietnamese cooking and usually feature in versions of this refreshing salad. I wanted to add something extra to serve alongside, and found inspiration for the crispy fried beef from my local Vietnamese restaurant. It's substantial enough for a light lunch or can be served as a starter. Add halved cherry tomatoes and lightly blanched green beans for extra colour and texture. Green papayas, Thai basil and crispy fried shallots can all be found in good Asian food stores and markets. The recipe makes possibly more beef than you need, but it's not really worth the bother to make less. Any leftovers will keep for up to a week in an airtight container in the fridge and can be served with noodles or egg fried rice, or just as a snack.

SERVES 4

For the beef

500G BEEF SKIRT, IN ONE PIECE

1 TABLESPOON DARK SOY SAUCE

2 TABLESPOONS LIGHT SOY SAUCE

1 ROUNDED TABLESPOON PALM OR LIGHT BROWN SUGAR

1 LEMONGRASS STALK, TRIMMED

2 GARLIC CLOVES, SLICED

3CM PIECE OF FRESH GINGER, SHREDDED

1 LARGE RED CHILLI, SLICED

To finish

2 GARLIC CLOVES, ROUGHLY CHOPPED

4CM PIECE OF FRESH GINGER, ROUGHLY CHOPPED

2 TEASPOONS PALM OR SOFT LIGHT BROWN SUGAR

1 TEASPOON GROUND CORIANDER

A GOOD PINCH OF GROUND CUMIN

4 TABLESPOONS COCONUT MILK

A PINCH OF SALT

2 TABLESPOONS SUNFLOWER OIL

4 TEASPOONS TAMARIND PASTE

SQUEEZE OF LIME JUICE

For the salad

1 MEDIUM GREEN PAPAYA

1 RED ONION, FINELY SLICED

A GOOD HANDFUL OF BEANSPROUTS, RINSED

1 GARLIC CLOVE, PEELED

2 RED BIRD'S EYE CHILLIES, ROUGHLY CHOPPED

1 LEMONGRASS STALK, TRIMMED AND SLICED

2–3 TEASPOONS PALM OR SOFT LIGHT BROWN SUGAR

2–3 TABLESPOONS FISH SAUCE, OR TO TASTE

JUICE OF 2 LIMES, OR TO TASTE

A HANDFUL OF THAI BASIL OR MINT, LEAVES TORN

A HANDFUL OF CORIANDER LEAVES

2 TABLESPOONS CRISPY ASIAN SHALLOTS (OPTIONAL)

2 TABLESPOONS ROUGHLY CHOPPED SALTED PEANUTS

Preheat the oven to 180°C/gas mark 4.

Put the beef into a flameproof casserole with a tight-fitting lid. Mix together the soy sauces and sugar and pour over the beef. Bruise the lemongrass stalk with the back of a knife and cut in half, then add to the pan with the garlic, ginger and chilli and mix well with your hands. Add enough cold water to half cover the meat and slowly bring to the boil. Cover with the lid and cook in the oven for 1 hour or until the meat is very tender and will shred easily. Leave to cool in the broth, then drain and chill for a couple of hours or overnight.

Using your hands, pull the beef into long shreds and place in a large bowl. Using a pestle and mortar, pound the garlic and ginger with the sugar and spices until smooth. Add to the beef along with the coconut milk and salt. Mix, using clean hands, until thoroughly combined.

Heat the oil in a large frying pan, add the beef mixture and fry over a low–medium heat until dry and crisp, stirring frequently. This will take a good 20 minutes and shouldn't be rushed. Add the tamarind paste and lime juice and cook for a further minute. Leave to cool to room temperature while you prepare the salad.

Peel the papaya, cut in half, scoop out any seeds, then cut into fine matchsticks using a sharp knife or mandolin and tip into a bowl. Add the red onion and beansprouts. Using the pestle and mortar, pound together the garlic,

chillies, lemongrass and sugar until finely mashed and combined. Add the fish sauce and lime juice, taste and add more sugar, fish sauce or lime juice to balance the flavours. Pour over the salad, add the herbs and mix to combine. Spoon onto serving plates, scatter with the crispy shallots, if using, and peanuts and serve immediately with a generous helping of the beef.

Mango and Chilli Hot Sauce

This sauce is great as a dip for potato wedges or fries and is also good served with barbecued sausages or burgers. In fact, I tend to use it whenever I would use tomato ketchup. I have opted for the larger, medium-hot red chillies here, which I think give a good depth and balance of heat, but feel free to add a couple of bird's eye chillies if your chilli tolerance levels are on the high side. But just remember that it's not big or clever to make a chilli sauce that's too hot to eat and brings you or your guests out in a sweat and renders you speechless.

MAKES 2–3 JARS

400G LARGE, MEDIUM-HOT RED CHILLIES

5 FAT GARLIC CLOVES, ROUGHLY CHOPPED

50G FRESH GINGER, ROUGHLY CHOPPED

1 FAT OR 2 SLIM LEMONGRASS STALKS, TOUGH OUTER LEAVES DISCARDED, INNER STALKS TRIMMED AND SLICED

250ML CIDER OR RICE VINEGAR

200–225G SOFT LIGHT BROWN SUGAR

2 STAR ANISE

1 TEASPOON SEA SALT FLAKES

4 LARGE RIPE MANGOES

2 TEASPOONS FISH SAUCE

JUICE OF 1 LIME

Equipment

2–3 X 450G JAM JARS

Slice the stalk off each chilli, then cut in half lengthways and roughly chop the flesh – don't remove the seeds. Tip into the bowl of a food processor with the garlic, ginger and lemongrass and whizz until finely chopped. Using a rubber spatula, scoop the mixture into a large, stainless steel saucepan. Wash the food processor bowl and blade immediately to prevent them becoming chilli-tainted.

Add the vinegar, sugar, star anise and salt to the pan and place over a medium heat. Bring to a simmer, stirring frequently to dissolve the sugar, and cook for 5–10 minutes.

Meanwhile, slice off the cheeks – the rounded fleshy pieces either side of the thin stone – of each mango. Using the tip of the knife, cut a grid into the cut side of each mango cheek all the way down to (but not through) the skin. Push the mango cheek outwards so that the skin is inverted and the flesh exposed in perfect little cubes. It's now easy to slice off all the flesh. Slice the skin away from the mango stone section and then carefully slice the mango flesh away from the stone. Add all the mango flesh to the pan with the fish sauce and lime juice, stir well and continue to cook for about 40 minutes until very soft and the sauce starts to thicken to the consistency of ketchup. I find it helps to have the extractor fan on to keep the chilli fumes to a minimum.

Slide the pan off the heat, leave to cool for a couple of minutes and then whizz the sauce until it's as smooth as possible, either in the food processor or a blender or using a stick blender. Push the sauce through a fine-mesh nylon sieve and pour into the warm sterilised jars (see page 132), seal with the lids and leave until cold before labelling and storing in the fridge. It will keep for up to 3 months.

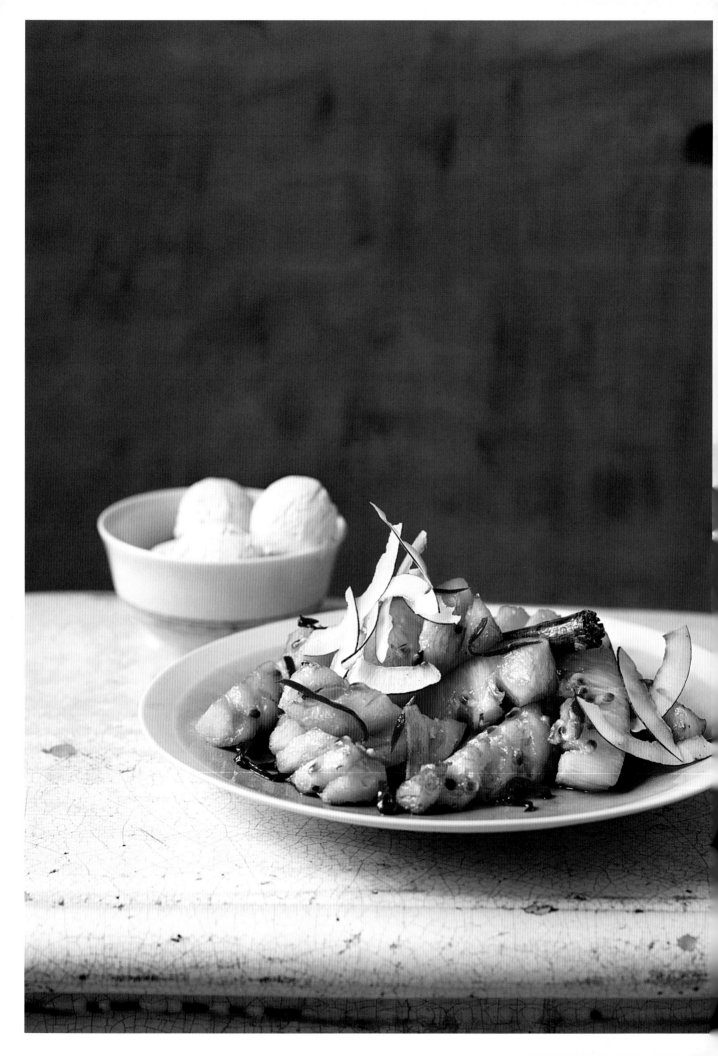

Roasted Chilli-spiked Pineapple

The first time I made this, I greedily ate almost the entire pineapple, with my fingers, standing up and moments after pulling it out of the oven. I could barely wait for it to cool – the intense aroma of pineapple was speaking to me. The sliced red chilli gives the pineapple and its resulting syrup a warming glow without blowing your socks off. And the dark rum just rounds things off, but obviously leave it out if children are involved.

SERVES 4–6

1 LARGE RIPE PINEAPPLE

1 LARGE MEDIUM-HOT RED CHILLI, SLICED

5CM PIECE OF FRESH GINGER, SLICED

1 STAR ANISE

1 SMALL CINNAMON STICK

4 TABLESPOONS LIGHT MUSCOVADO SUGAR

A PINCH OF SEA SALT FLAKES

JUICE OF 1 LARGE JUICY LIME

3 PASSION FRUIT, HALVED

2 TABLESPOONS DARK RUM (OPTIONAL)

This method of preparing a pineapple sounds tricky but is in fact brilliant. Pineapples are prepared in this way on street-side fruit stalls all over South East Asia and I was first shown it by Lizzie Mabbott, a fellow food writer with an amazing knowledge of Asian cooking. Now that I've mastered it, I'll never go back to trying to gouge out the prickly 'eyes' from the pineapple with the point of a knife.

Line a baking tray with baking parchment or foil.

Slice the leafy top and the tough bottom stalk end off the pineapple so that you have a flat underside. Stand the pineapple on its flat bottom and, using a long, sharp knife, cut the skin in strips from the pineapple, working from top to bottom and using a sawing action. Now take a look at the pineapple and you'll notice that the fibrous 'eyes' go around the pineapple in helter-skelter diagonal lines from top to bottom. Pick one of the eyes at the top of the pineapple as your starting point and, using a smaller sharp knife, make a neat wedge cut in a line diagonally down the pineapple on either side of the eyes, cutting them out neatly. Repeat with all the eyes. What you should end up with is a neat barrel-shaped pineapple with grooves running down the outside of the flesh in a corkscrew fashion.

Cut the pineapple in half through the core from top to bottom. Cut in half again to give even-sized quarters, then slice out the hard core from each quarter and cut each quarter in half again to make eight neat wedges. Arrange on the lined baking tray. Add the chilli, ginger, star anise, cinnamon stick, sugar and salt. Mix gently with your hands to thoroughly coat and set aside for 20–30 minutes so that the sugar dissolves and the pineapple starts to release its juice. Meanwhile, preheat the oven to 200°C/gas mark 6.

Slide the baking tray into the hot oven and bake the pineapple for about 30 minutes until tender and golden at the edges. You may need to carefully turn the pineapple pieces over halfway through to ensure that they cook and start to caramelise evenly.

Remove from the oven and immediately pour over the lime juice. Scoop the seeds and juice from the passion fruit halves into the tray and add the rum, if using. Gently turn the pineapple over in the juices to coat thoroughly and leave to cool for 5 minutes before serving, preferably with Toasted Coconut Ice Cream (see page 168).

Hummingbird Cake

I never tire of saying it, but you really do need to use ripe fruit for this recipe. A pineapple that is super-sweet and juicy and bananas with skins that are mottled with brown spots will result in a moist and truly flavoursome cake. Hummingbird cake hails from the southern States of America and is more often than not made using canned crushed pineapple, which you could use here at a pinch. Using fresh, though, gives you the perfect excuse to use the remaining pineapple half to make the candied pineapple wafers. You also have the option of using coconut crystals in place of brown sugar; both this and the coconut nectar (available from health-food stores and suppliers) have a warm, caramel flavour with just a hint of coconut, making them ideal for this recipe.

SERVES 8-10

350G PLAIN FLOUR

1 TEASPOON BAKING POWDER

1 TEASPOON BICARBONATE OF SODA

1 TEASPOON GROUND CINNAMON

¼ TEASPOON MIXED SPICE

A PINCH OF SALT

125G CASTER SUGAR

125G COCONUT CRYSTALS OR SOFT LIGHT
BROWN SUGAR

250G RIPE PINEAPPLE FLESH (PREPARED
WEIGHT – ABOUT ½ MEDIUM PINEAPPLE)

2 LARGE RIPE BANANAS

75G COCONUT OIL OR UNSALTED BUTTER,
PLUS EXTRA BUTTER FOR GREASING

125ML SUNFLOWER OIL

3 MEDIUM EGGS, LIGHTLY BEATEN

1 TEASPOON VANILLA EXTRACT

75G PECANS, CHOPPED

50G DESICCATED COCONUT

For the pineapple wafers

50G CASTER SUGAR

JUICE OF ½ LIME

2CM PIECE FRESH GINGER, ROUGHLY
CHOPPED

2 TABLESPOONS DARK RUM

25ML WATER

½ MEDIUM RIPE PINEAPPLE

Preheat the oven to 180°C/gas mark 4. Grease and line the base of each cake tin with a disc of greased baking parchment.

Sift the flour, baking powder, bicarbonate of soda, spices and salt into a large mixing bowl. Add the sugars and mix well to combine. Make a well in the middle and set aside.

Finely chop the pineapple and mash the bananas. Gently melt the coconut oil or butter in a small saucepan over a low heat, or in the microwave on a low setting, and add the sunflower oil. Pour into the middle of the dry ingredients, add the eggs and vanilla and beat until almost smooth. Add the pineapple, bananas, pecans and desiccated coconut and stir until smooth.

Divide the mixture evenly between the prepared cake tins and bake on the middle shelf of the oven for 25–30 minutes or until well risen, golden brown and a skewer inserted into the middle of the cakes comes out clean. Leave to rest in the tins for 2–3 minutes and then carefully turn out onto a wire rack to cool completely.

For the pineapple wafers, preheat the oven to 110°C/gas mark ¼. Cover a solid baking tray with non-stick baking parchment.

Combine all the ingredients, except the pineapple, in a small saucepan and heat gently to dissolve the sugar. Bring to the boil and then simmer for 30 seconds. Remove from the heat.

Peel the pineapple and, using a long, sharp knife or a mandolin, slice into wafer-thin slices. Dip each slice into the rum syrup and arrange in a single layer on the lined baking tray. Bake on the middle shelf of the oven for around 1 hour until slightly golden and crisp, turning the slices over after 30 minutes and the tray around to ensure that they dry evenly. Lay the slices on a wire rack until cold and crisp.

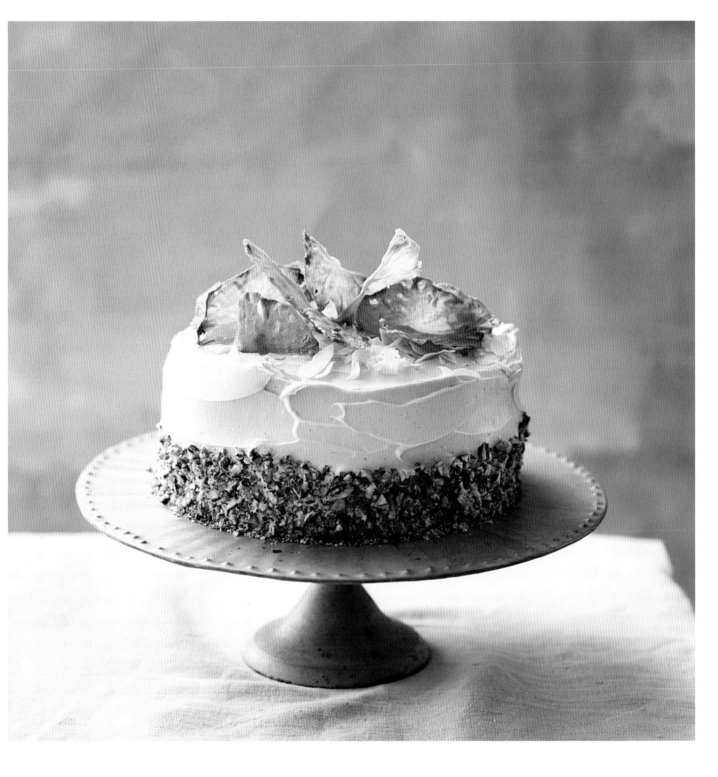

For the frosting

500G FULL-FAT CREAM CHEESE

2 TABLESPOONS COCONUT NECTAR
OR CLEAR HONEY

¼ TEASPOON GROUND CINNAMON

100G PECANS, FINELY CHOPPED

50G FLAKED COCONUT

Equipment

3 X 20CM ROUND CAKE TINS

For the frosting, beat the cream cheese, nectar or honey and cinnamon together in a bowl until smooth and thickened. Place one cake layer on a serving plate or cake stand and spread with 2 tablespoons of the frosting. Top with a second cake layer and more frosting. Carefully add the third cake and cover the top and sides with the remaining frosting, spreading it evenly and smoothly with a palette knife. Scatter the sides with the pecans and the top with the flaked coconut and pineapple wafers.

Mango and Passion Fruit Cake

This cake is a veritable ray of sunshine on a plate. Be sure to use juicy, ripe mangoes. They won't necessarily be as easy to slice as under-ripe fruit but will taste vastly superior. Try to arrange the slices as neatly as possible for a picture-perfect result.

SERVES 8

275G CASTER SUGAR

225G UNSALTED BUTTER, SOFTENED, PLUS
EXTRA FOR GREASING

1½ TEASPOONS VANILLA EXTRACT OR
VANILLA BEAN PASTE

3 LARGE PASSION FRUIT, HALVED

2 LARGE OR 3 SMALL RIPE MANGOES

4 MEDIUM EGGS, LIGHTLY BEATEN

225G PLAIN FLOUR

2 TEASPOONS BAKING POWDER

A PINCH OF FINE SEA SALT

2 TABLESPOONS SOURED CREAM, AT ROOM
TEMPERATURE

Equipment

20CM ROUND HEAVY-BOTTOMED CAKE TIN

Preheat the oven to 180°C/gas mark 4 and grease the base and sides of the cake tin.

Heat 100g of the sugar with 2 tablespoons cold water in a small saucepan over a low heat to dissolve the sugar. Bring to the boil and continue to cook without stirring until the sugar has turned an amber caramel colour. Add 50g of the butter and ½ teaspoon of the vanilla and swirl the pan to incorporate evenly. Immediately pour into the prepared cake tin, covering the base with an even layer of caramel, then leave to cool slightly. Scoop the seeds and juice from the halves of 1 passion fruit over the top of the caramel.

Peel the mangoes, slice off the 'cheeks' either side of the narrow stone and thinly slice the flesh. Slice the remaining mango flesh from around the stone. Arrange the slices neatly, slightly overlapping, over the cold, hard caramel.

Using a free-standing mixer, cream the remaining butter and sugar together until pale, light and fluffy. Gradually add the beaten eggs, mixing well between each addition and scraping down the sides of the bowl with a rubber spatula from time to time. Sift in the flour, baking powder and salt, add the seeds and juice of the remaining 2 passion fruit and the soured cream and mix again until smooth and thoroughly combined.

Carefully spoon the cake mixture over the mango slices and spread level using a palette knife or the back of the spoon. Bake on the middle shelf of the oven for 50 minutes–1 hour or until a skewer inserted into the middle of the cake comes out clean. If it's browning too quickly, reduce the oven temperature to 170°C/gas mark 3 or loosely cover the top of the cake with baking parchment. Leave to cool in the tin for 5 minutes before turning out onto a serving dish.

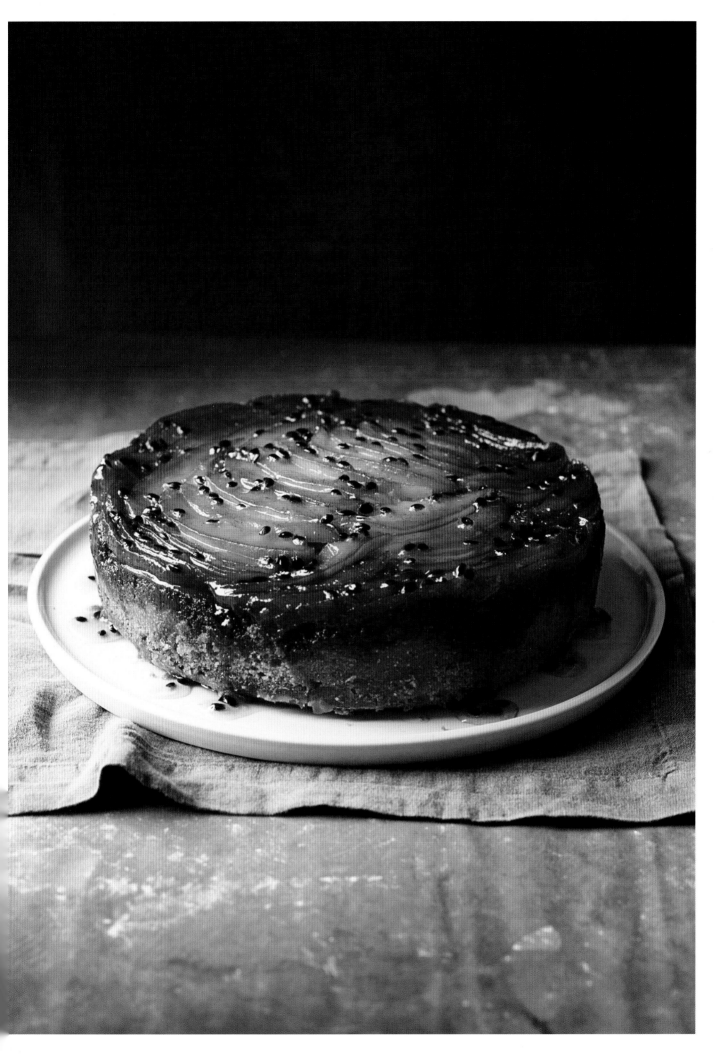

Mango and Passion Fruit Sorbet

Something this easy and delicious is a winner in my book. If you can find Alphonso mangoes, which have a tender, juicy and vibrant, almost egg yolk-orange flesh and an intense sweetness, then use them. You may want to increase the lime juice slightly if your mangoes are super-sweet – but just enough to balance the flavour. You could also add some freshly grated ginger or a tiny amount of fresh red chilli for extra oomph. If you want to make the sorbet without an ice-cream maker, freeze the mixture in a plastic freezer box for 2 hours, whisk it to break up the ice crystals and repeat the freezing and whisking process a further three times until the sorbet is firm. You could then whizz the sorbet in a food processor to lighten it further. Using an ice-cream maker, however, will result in a very light, almost creamy sorbet.

SERVES 8

3 MEDIUM OR 2 LARGE RIPE MANGOES

JUICE OF 1 LIME

3 LARGE PASSION FRUIT

250G CASTER SUGAR

A PINCH OF SALT

Equipment

ICE-CREAM MAKER (OR SEE RECIPE INTRODUCTION)

PLASTIC FREEZER BOX

Peel the mangoes and slice all the flesh into a blender goblet and add the lime juice. Blend the fruit until silky smooth and pour into a bowl. Cut the passion fruit in half and scoop the juice and seeds into a sieve placed over the bowl. Push all the pulp and juice from the passion fruit into the mango purée and discard the seeds.

Tip the sugar into a medium saucepan, add 250ml cold water and the salt and bring slowly to the boil to dissolve the sugar. Simmer for 2 minutes, then remove from the heat and leave to cool for 15 minutes before adding to the fruit. Stir until combined and leave until cold before thoroughly chilling in the fridge for at least 2 hours but preferably overnight.

Churn the mixture in an ice-cream maker according to the manufacturer's instructions. Transfer to a plastic freezer box, cover and freeze until firm before serving.

Toasted Coconut Ice Cream

This is perfect when served alongside the Roasted Chilli-spiked Pineapple on page 163 or with Mango and Passion Fruit Sorbet, above, but is equally delicious when drizzled with a warm dark chocolate sauce.

SERVES 6–8

50G DESICCATED COCONUT

250ML FULL-FAT MILK

250ML COCONUT MILK

4 LARGE EGG YOLKS

100G GOLDEN CASTER SUGAR, OR 50G COCONUT CRYSTALS AND 50G GOLDEN CASTER SUGAR

1 TEASPOON VANILLA EXTRACT OR VANILLA BEAN PASTE

200ML DOUBLE CREAM

2 TABLESPOONS DARK RUM (OPTIONAL)

FRESHLY GRATED NUTMEG

Equipment

FINE-MESH NYLON SIEVE

ICE-CREAM MAKER

PLASTIC FREEZER BOX

Tip the coconut into a frying pan and toast over a low–medium heat until golden brown, shaking the pan regularly to prevent it scorching. Tip into a bowl and leave to cool.

Heat the milk and coconut milk in a saucepan over a medium heat to just below boiling point. Meanwhile, whisk the egg yolks, sugar and vanilla together in a bowl until very pale and thick. Add the hot milk mixture in a steady stream, whisking constantly until smooth. Return to the pan and cook over a low heat, stirring constantly,

until it thickens enough to coat the back of the spoon, but don't allow it to boil or the eggs may scramble. Strain through a fine-mesh nylon sieve into a clean bowl. Add the cream, rum, if using, and a good grating of nutmeg. Leave to cool completely, then chill thoroughly for a good couple of hours, preferably overnight.

Churn the mixture in an ice-cream maker according to the manufacturer's instructions. Stir in the toasted coconut, then spoon into a plastic freezer box, cover and freeze until required.

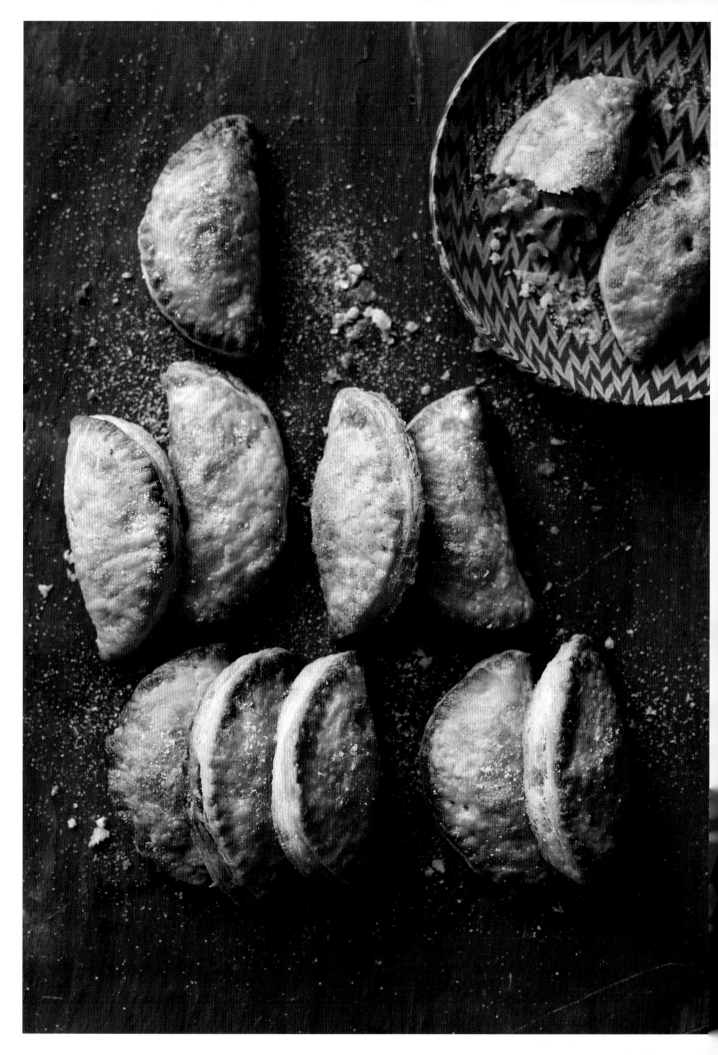

Pineapple Empanadas

This recipe for sweet empanadas uses the same cream cheese pastry as my Apple Tarte Tatin on page 208. The buttery, flaky pastry is not only a doddle to make but perfectly complements the sweet, slightly spiced pineapple filling. These empanadas are irresistible and are best eaten while still warm – as my editor Judith and photographer Tara will testify. Coconut or vanilla ice cream would be delicious served alongside.

MAKES ABOUT 16

1 QUANTITY OF CREAM CHEESE PASTRY DOUGH (SEE PAGE 208), CHILLED

PLAIN FLOUR, FOR DUSTING

For the filling

1 MEDIUM RIPE PINEAPPLE, PEELED, CORED AND ROUGHLY CHOPPED

JUICE OF 1 LIME

2 TABLESPOONS LIGHT MUSCOVADO SUGAR

A GENEROUS PINCH OF ANCHO CHILLI POWDER

1 TEASPOON GROUND CINNAMON

1 TABLESPOON CASTER SUGAR

2 TABLESPOONS MILK

Equipment

11–12CM PLAIN COOKIE CUTTER

Place the pineapple, lime juice, muscovado sugar, chilli powder and a good pinch of the cinnamon in a sauté pan and cook over a low–medium heat until the fruit is tender, slightly jammy and caramelised. Remove from the heat and leave to cool.

Preheat the oven to 180°C/gas mark 4 and line two baking trays with baking parchment. In a small bowl, mix the remaining cinnamon with the caster sugar.

Lightly dust the work surface with flour and roll out the chilled pastry dough to a thickness of 2mm. Using the cutter, stamp out as many discs from the pastry as you can, re-rolling the trimmings and stamping out more. Lay the discs out on the work surface and spoon 1 dessertspoonful of the filling into the middle of each. Brush the edges with a little milk and fold the pastry over the filling to make half-moon shapes, completely encasing the filling. Press the edges to seal and arrange on the lined baking trays. Press the tines of a fork around the edges of each empanada, brush the tops with milk and sprinkle with the cinnamon sugar.

Bake on the middle shelf of the oven for about 20 minutes until golden brown and crisp.

Try swapping or upping the spices in the pineapple filling – a pinch of ground cardamom or aniseed would be quite lovely. As for the ancho chilli powder, this is available in good delis or online and has a sweet, fruity smokiness to it rather than a head-popping chilli heat.

Goat's Milk Labneh with Carrot, Beetroot and Pomegranate Salad

Labneh is simply natural yogurt that has been seasoned and strained overnight through muslin until it becomes like a soft cheese. I like to use goat's milk yogurt as it has a more grassy taste than regular yogurt which contrasts deliciously with the sweet, roasted carrots and beetroots and sharp pomegranate seeds. You could also add a crushed clove of garlic and a pinch of ground cumin seeds to pep up the labneh, and of course use regular yogurt if you prefer.

SERVES 4–6

500G FULL-FAT GOAT'S MILK YOGURT

A BUNCH OF MIXED SMALL HERITAGE CARROTS

A BUNCH OF MIXED SMALL BEETROOTS

3 TABLESPOONS OLIVE OIL

3 GARLIC CLOVES, UNPEELED

1 SPRIG OF THYME, LEAVES PICKED

2 TABLESPOONS ROUGHLY CHOPPED FLAT-LEAF PARSLEY

1 TABLESPOON ROUGHLY CHOPPED MINT

SEEDS FROM 1 POMEGRANATE

50G NIBBED PISTACHIOS

1 TABLESPOON POMEGRANATE MOLASSES

1–2 TABLESPOONS PISTACHIO OR EXTRA VIRGIN OLIVE OIL

½ TEASPOON GROUND SUMAC

SALT AND FRESHLY GROUND BLACK PEPPER

Equipment

FINE-MESH NYLON SIEVE

PIECE OF CLEAN MUSLIN

Season the yogurt with salt and black pepper. Line a fine-mesh nylon sieve with the muslin and scoop the seasoned yogurt into the lined sieve. Suspend the sieve over a bowl, cover with clingfilm and leave in the fridge for 24 hours to allow the water to drain from the yogurt.

Preheat the oven to 190°C/gas mark 5. Scrub the carrots and beetroots and remove the stalks and leaves. Cut any large carrots in half and tip into a roasting tin, drizzle with the oil and season with salt and black pepper. Tuck the garlic cloves amongst the carrots, scatter with the thyme and roast on the middle shelf of the oven for about 30 minutes, depending on size, until tender.

Cook the unpeeled beetroots in a saucepan of boiling salted water until tender, drain and leave until cool enough to handle. Peel and cut into bite-sized wedges.

Tip the carrots and beetroots into a bowl, add the chopped herbs, squeeze in the roasted garlic from its skin and season with salt and black pepper. Mix the veggies gently using your hands and arrange on a serving platter. Dot the labneh over the top and scatter with the pomegranate seeds and pistachios. Drizzle over the pomegranate molasses and pistachio or olive oil and season with a sprinkling of the sumac. Serve immediately.

Chocolate and Pomegranate Pots with Cocoa and Almond Nib Wafers

These chocolate pots are simple yet elegant, the pomegranate giving an intriguing twist to a classic dinner party dessert. I like to serve something crisp alongside rich, creamy desserts and these cocoa nib wafers do the job nicely. The delicate biscuits will soften in damp air or humidity, so make them on the day you plan to serve them and, once cooled, store in an airtight container between layers of baking parchment; the recipe makes around 20.

SERVES 6

2 LARGE POMEGRANATES

2 TEASPOONS CASTER SUGAR

200G DARK CHOCOLATE, 70% COCOA SOLIDS, FINELY CHOPPED

325ML DOUBLE CREAM

A PINCH OF SALT

½ TEASPOON VANILLA EXTRACT

1 MEDIUM EGG YOLK, LIGHTLY BEATEN

For the wafers

75G UNSALTED BUTTER

1 TABLESPOON CLEAR HONEY

100G CASTER SUGAR

40G PLAIN FLOUR

50G COCOA NIBS

30G FLAKED ALMONDS

A PINCH OF SALT

Cut one of the pomegranates in half and press the fruit though an orange juicer to extract as much juice as possible from the seeds. Pour the juice into a small saucepan, add the sugar and stir to dissolve. Bring the juice to the boil over a medium heat and continue to cook for about 1 minute until reduced by half and thickened and syrupy.

Tip the chocolate into a bowl. In a separate saucepan, bring the cream with the salt and vanilla to the boil and then simmer for 20 seconds before pouring over the chocolate. Add half the pomegranate syrup (reserve the remainder for serving) and, using a rubber spatula, stir gently until the chocolate has melted and the ganache is silky smooth. Add the egg yolk and mix until combined. Divide the mixture between six small glasses or pots. Leave to cool and then cover with clingfilm and chill in the fridge until set.

To make the wafers, melt the butter with the honey and sugar in a small saucepan over a low–medium heat. Remove from the heat and leave to cool for 3–4 minutes before adding the remaining ingredients. Mix until thoroughly combined and then leave for at least 1 hour until firm. The dough can be made, covered and chilled up to 24 hours before you plan on baking the wafers.

Preheat the oven to 170°C/gas mark 3. Line two large baking trays with baking parchment.

You will need to bake the wafers in small batches of 4 or 5 at a time. Spoon small cherry-sized balls of the dough onto each lined baking tray and flatten into a neat disc using either your fingers or a palette knife. Bake on the middle shelf of the oven for 6–7 minutes or until golden brown and bubbling. Remove from the oven and leave to cool and harden on the trays.

To serve, divide the reserved syrup between the pots, top with the seeds from the remaining pomegranate and serve with the wafers.

Turkish Pide with Lamb and Pomegranate Seeds

Pide is the Turkish equivalent of pizza, and these examples are topped with a delicious combination of aromatic spiced lamb mince, salty feta, smoky peppers and a final contrasting flourish of fresh, juicy pomegranate seeds. They are ideal for lunch or supper, and can be knocked up in very little time, especially if you prepare the lamb topping in advance.

MAKES 8 PIDE

For the topping

1 TABLESPOON OLIVE OIL

1 ONION, FINELY CHOPPED

2 GARLIC CLOVES, CRUSHED

1 TEASPOON GROUND CUMIN

½ TEASPOON GROUND CORIANDER

½ TEASPOON CAYENNE PEPPER

A PINCH OF GROUND ALLSPICE

¼ TEASPOON GROUND CINNAMON

¼ TEASPOON DRIED OREGANO

400G LEAN LAMB MINCE

200G CANNED OR FRESH CHOPPED TOMATOES

1 TABLESPOON POMEGRANATE MOLASSES

A PINCH OF SUGAR

100G ROASTED RED PEPPERS FROM A JAR (DRAINED WEIGHT), SLICED INTO STRIPS

125G FETA, CRUMBLED

2 TEASPOONS KALONJI (NIGELLA) SEEDS

SEEDS FROM 1 POMEGRANATE

1 ROUNDED TABLESPOON CHOPPED FLAT-LEAF PARSLEY

½ TEASPOON GROUND SUMAC

SALT AND FRESHLY GROUND BLACK PEPPER

For the dough

350G STRONG WHITE FLOUR, PLUS EXTRA FOR DUSTING

7G FAST-ACTION/EASY-BLEND DRIED YEAST

A PINCH OF CASTER SUGAR

A GOOD PINCH OF SEA SALT

2 TABLESPOONS OLIVE OIL, PLUS EXTRA

First begin preparing the topping. Heat the olive oil in a large frying pan, add the onion and cook over a medium heat until tender but not coloured. Add the garlic, spices and oregano and cook for a further minute. Tip in the lamb and cook for about 5 minutes on a medium–high heat until browned. Add the chopped tomatoes, pomegranate molasses and sugar and season with salt and black pepper. Cook for a further 20 minutes until the meat is tender and most of the moisture from the tomatoes has been cooked off. Remove from the heat, spoon off any excess fat and leave to cool while you prepare the dough.

Tip the flour into the bowl of a free-standing mixer fitted with a dough hook. Add the yeast, sugar and salt and mix well until combined. Make a well in the middle and add 200–225ml warm water and the olive oil. Mix on medium speed for about 8 minutes until the dough is silky smooth and elastic. Turn out onto a work surface and shape into a ball. Place in a lightly oiled bowl, cover with clingfilm and leave in a warm place for about 1 hour or until doubled in size.

Preheat the oven to 200°C/gas mark 6 and line 2 large baking trays with baking parchment.

Turn the dough out onto a lightly floured work surface, knead lightly and divide into 8 even-sized pieces. Roll each piece out into an oval shape roughly the same size as a pitta bread and about 3mm thick. Divide the lamb mixture between the dough shapes, spooning it into the middle of dough and leaving a border all round. Twist the ends of the dough together so that the dough forms a 'boat' shape that encases the lamb. Scatter the roasted pepper strips over the lamb along with the feta. Drizzle the pide with olive oil, sprinkle with the kalonji (nigella) seeds and bake on the middle shelf of the oven for about 20 minutes until the dough is puffed and golden brown.

Generously scatter the hot pide with the pomegranate seeds and chopped parsley, season with the sumac and serve immediately with pickled green chillies.

Beef Short Ribs Braised in Pomegranate

This is one of my new favourite dishes, making the most of pomegranate in a triple hit of juice, molasses and fresh seeds. I'll admit that I have a tendency to be a lazy cook – I often choose dishes that require the minimum of effort yet give a huge return in terms of flavour and deliciousness. Beef short ribs are ideal for just such a choice, as they almost look after themselves in the oven while they gently cook to melting tenderness in a pool of spiced fruity juices. The dish can also be half or fully prepared in advance; the ribs should be marinated overnight for the best outcome. Serve simply with some steamed rice and crisp garlicky greens.

SERVES 4 GENEROUSLY

2KG BEEF SHORT RIBS

2 TEASPOONS CUMIN SEEDS

2 TEASPOONS CORIANDER SEEDS

1 ROUNDED TEASPOON ANCHO OR CHIPOTLE CHILLI POWDER

½ TEASPOON DRIED OREGANO

2 RED ONIONS, SLICED

3 GARLIC CLOVES, BRUISED

1 CINNAMON STICK

2 TABLESPOONS OLIVE OIL

1 TABLESPOON TOMATO PURÉE

500ML UNSWEETENED POMEGRANATE JUICE

500ML GOOD RICH BEEF STOCK

2 TABLESPOONS POMEGRANATE MOLASSES

1–2 TEASPOONS SOFT LIGHT BROWN SUGAR

SEEDS FROM 1 POMEGRANATE

2 TABLESPOONS CHOPPED FLAT-LEAF PARSLEY

2 TABLESPOONS CHOPPED CORIANDER

1 RED CHILLI, FINELY CHOPPED

SALT AND FRESHLY GROUND BLACK PEPPER

Slice the beef into individual ribs and place in a large bowl.

Heat a small frying pan over a medium heat, add the cumin and coriander seeds and toast for a minute or so until smoking and fragrant. Grind the seeds using a pestle and mortar, then mix in the chilli powder, oregano and a good seasoning of salt and black pepper. Tip over the ribs and add the onions, garlic and cinnamon stick. Mix well using your hands, making sure that the spices are really well rubbed into the meat. Cover with clingfilm and leave to marinate in the fridge overnight.

Preheat the oven to 150°C/gas mark 2. Remove the ribs from the bowl, scraping off the onions and garlic and reserving them. Heat 1 tablespoon of the olive oil in a large frying pan, add the ribs and brown well on all sides. Remove from the pan and transfer to a flameproof casserole. Add the remaining tablespoon of oil to the frying pan and cook the onions and garlic until soft but not coloured, stirring frequently to cook evenly. Add the tomato purée, mix well and cook for a further minute. Pour the pomegranate juice and stock into the pan, bring to the boil and stir well to incorporate any browned bits on the base of the pan. Pour over the ribs and bring back to the boil. Cover with the lid and cook on the middle shelf of the oven for about 2 hours until the meat is tender and almost falling off the bone.

Using a slotted spoon, remove the ribs from the casserole, cover with foil and keep warm. Leave the sauce to rest and cool for 15 minutes and then spoon off any excess fat on top. Place the casserole over a medium heat, add the pomegranate molasses and reduce the sauce by half until thickened and glossy. Taste and add sugar, salt and black pepper as needed. Return the ribs to the casserole, scatter with the pomegranate seeds, herbs and chilli and serve immediately.

Gulab Jamun with Pomegranate and Pistachio

When travelling through India a few years ago, I used to treat myself to a gulab jamun whenever I saw them – often from a street vendor and served in a little banana leaf bowl. These Indian doughnut milk balls are deep-fried to a golden brown colour and then completely drenched in a fragrant cardamom and rose syrup. I serve them with fresh, sharp pomegranate seeds to contrast the sweetness, and pistachios for a pop of colour and crunch.

SERVES 8–10

1 LITRE SUNFLOWER OIL, FOR DEEP-FRYING

200G DRIED MILK POWDER

50G PLAIN FLOUR

A PINCH OF BICARBONATE OF SODA

75ML FULL-FAT MILK, PLUS EXTRA IF NEEDED

75G NATURAL YOGURT

2 TABLESPOONS MELTED CLARIFIED BUTTER

For the syrup

350G CASTER SUGAR

6 GREEN CARDAMOM PODS

1 CINNAMON STICK

1–2 TEASPOONS ROSEWATER

2 TEASPOONS FOOD-GRADE DRIED ROSE PETALS (OPTIONAL)

To serve

40G NIBBED PISTACHIOS

SEEDS FROM 1 POMEGRANATE

Equipment

SUGAR THERMOMETER

Start by making the syrup. Tip the sugar and 500ml of cold water into a large saucepan. Bruise the cardamom pods using a pestle and mortar and add to the pan with the cinnamon stick. Bring slowly to the boil to dissolve the sugar, then simmer for 2 minutes. Slide off the heat and stir in the rosewater and dried rose petals – use the rosewater cautiously, as it can be overpowering and vary in strength.

Pour the sunflower oil into a large pan, wok or deep-fat fryer, pop a thermometer into the pan and heat the oil to 150°C.

While the oil is coming up to temperature, prepare the gulab jamun. In a large mixing bowl, mix together the milk powder, flour and bicarbonate of soda. Make a well in the centre and add the milk, yogurt and all but 1 teaspoon of the clarified butter. Using your hand, quickly mix everything until smooth, adding a little extra milk if the mixture appears dry – it should be quite sticky but the milk powder will start to absorb the liquid as you mix. Working quickly, lightly grease the palm of your hands with a little of the reserved clarified butter, pinch off a walnut-sized nugget of dough and roll into a totally smooth ball in your hands. Place on a baking parchment-lined tray and repeat until all the dough has been used up – you should end up with 20–24 balls. Loosely cover the tray with a slightly damp clean tea towel.

Once the oil has reached 150°C, bring the syrup back to the boil and then remove from the heat. Carefully drop 4–5 balls at a time into the hot oil, maintaining the heat at a steady 150°C, and cook for about 5 minutes, turning so that they cook to an even deep, amber golden brown and have almost doubled in size. Using a slotted spoon, scoop the gulab from the oil, drain briefly on kitchen paper and then drop them into the hot syrup. If the syrup cools down, gently heat it without boiling. Leave to soak overnight at room temperature.

The next day, scoop out the cardamom pods, cinnamon stick and rose petals and serve the gulab jamun with a spoonful of the syrup, scattered with the nibbed pistachios and pomegranate seeds.

Malted Chocolate Banana Cake

This cake makes the most of those over-ripe bananas that I always seem to have idling in the fruit bowl, their condition making them perfect for baking; under-ripe bananas will give little or no flavour whatever you do to them. The cake keeps well in an airtight container and actually benefits from being baked the day before you plan on serving and frosting.

SERVES 10

200G UNSALTED BUTTER, SOFTENED, PLUS 1 TABLESPOON, MELTED, FOR GREASING

25G COCOA POWDER, PLUS 1 TABLESPOON FOR DUSTING

275G PLAIN FLOUR

25G MALTED MILK POWDER (OVALTINE)

2 TEASPOONS BAKING POWDER

½ TEASPOON BICARBONATE OF SODA

A GOOD PINCH OF FINE SEA SALT

4 MEDIUM, RIPE BANANAS

3 TABLESPOONS SOURED CREAM, AT ROOM TEMPERATURE

1 TEASPOON VANILLA EXTRACT

125G SOFT LIGHT BROWN SUGAR

100G CASTER SUGAR

4 LARGE EGGS, BEATEN

50G DARK CHOCOLATE, FINELY CHOPPED

For the frosting

100G SOFT LIGHT BROWN SUGAR

100G DARK MUSCOVADO SUGAR

75G UNSALTED BUTTER

125ML DOUBLE CREAM

50G DARK CHOCOLATE, CHOPPED

½ TEASPOON VANILLA EXTRACT

A LARGE PINCH OF SEA SALT

Equipment

2.5-LITRE BUNDT TIN

Preheat the oven to 180°C/gas mark 4. Use the melted butter to coat the inside of the tin, making sure that you grease all the creases and ridges thoroughly. Dust the inside of the tin with an even coating of the extra 1 tablespoon cocoa and tip out any excess.

Sift together the remaining cocoa, flour, malted milk powder, baking powder, bicarbonate of soda and salt. In a separate bowl, mash the bananas, then add the soured cream and vanilla extract and mix to combine.

Using a free-standing mixer, cream the butter and both sugars together until pale, light and fluffy. Gradually add the beaten eggs, mixing well between each addition and scraping down the sides of the bowl with a rubber spatula from time to time. Tip in the dry ingredients and banana mixture and mix until thoroughly combined. Add the chocolate and fold in using the spatula.

Spoon the mixture into the prepared tin, spread level and bake in the oven on the shelf just below the middle for 30–40 minutes until well risen and a wooden skewer inserted into the middle comes out clean. Leave the cake to rest in the tin for no more than 2 minutes and then carefully turn out onto a wire rack until completely cold.

To make the frosting, gently heat both sugars, butter and cream in a small saucepan to dissolve the sugar and melt the butter, then bring to the boil. Simmer for 30 seconds, remove from the heat and add the chocolate, vanilla and salt. Stir until the chocolate has melted and the sauce is silky smooth. Carefully spoon the sauce over the cold cake, allowing it to drizzle over the sides, and leave to set before serving.

Sticky Spiced Pork Belly and Watermelon

This recipe is inspired by a dish served at Fatty Crab, a Malayasian-inspired restaurant in New York, where Zakary Pelaccio's Watermelon Pickle and Crispy Pork is permanently on the menu. My version is much simplified, though no less yummy, the pork being marinated overnight before cooking rather than being marinated, braised and then fried. I've also done away with the pickled watermelon rind while still keeping the salad fresh and light. Chilling the melon before serving creates a refreshing contrast to the salty, spiced pork.

SERVES 4

3 GARLIC CLOVES, SLICED

5CM PIECE OF FRESH GINGER, SLICED

1 ROUNDED TEASPOON CHINESE FIVE-SPICE

2 TABLESPOONS DARK SOY SAUCE

2 TABLESPOONS CLEAR HONEY

2 TABLESPOONS CHINESE BLACK
RICE VINEGAR

1.5KG BONELESS PORK BELLY, SKIN SCORED

SEA SALT FLAKES

For the salad

½ FOOTBALL-SIZED WATERMELON, CHILLED,
SKINNED AND CUT INTO BITE-SIZED CUBES

4 SPRING ONIONS, SLICED

1 LARGE RED CHILLI, DESEEDED AND SLICED

4CM PIECE OF FRESH GINGER, CUT INTO FINE
MATCHSTICKS

3 TABLESPOONS SESAME OIL

2 TABLESPOONS SOY SAUCE

JUICE OF 1 LIME, PLUS EXTRA TO SERVE

2–3 TEASPOONS BLACK OR TOASTED WHITE
SESAME SEEDS

3 TABLESPOONS ROUGHLY CHOPPED
CORIANDER

Start by marinating the pork. Tip the garlic and ginger into a baking tray or shallow bowl that will fit the pork belly lying flat and snuggly. Add the five-spice, soy sauce, honey and vinegar and mix to combine. Lay the pork in the tray or bowl, skin-side uppermost, cover with clingfilm and leave to marinate overnight in the fridge.

The next day, line a roasting tin with a double thickness of foil and sit a roasting or wire rack on top. Remove the pork from the marinade, lay on top of the rack, skin-side uppermost, and leave for an hour at room temperature to dry the skin.

Preheat the oven to 220°C/gas mark 7. Sprinkle the pork skin lightly with sea salt flakes and roast for 20 minutes on the middle shelf of the oven. Reduce the temperature to 180°C/gas mark 4 and cook the pork for another hour until the skin has crisped and the meat is cooked through.

Meanwhile, for the salad, tip the prepared watermelon, spring onions, chilli and ginger into a bowl and use your hands to very gently mix. Combine the sesame oil, soy sauce and lime juice in a cup, but don't pour over the salad until just before serving, otherwise the watermelon will become soggy.

Once the pork is cooked, leave it to rest for 10 minutes and then cut into small bite-sized pieces. Pour the dressing over the salad and divide between serving plates. Arrange the pork on top, scatter with the sesame seeds and coriander and serve immediately with extra lime on the side.

Chargrilled Prawns with Watermelon and Feta

This is really a pimped-up Greek salad. Hot, sweet and spiced prawns are a wonderful contrast to chilled, juicy watermelon and salty feta. For best effect, serve this dish outside on a hot summer's day, with the prawns cooked on the barbecue if you should happen to have it lit already.

SERVES 3–4

16 RAW WHOLE TIGER PRAWNS

2 UNWAXED LEMONS

3 GARLIC CLOVES, SLICED

½–1 TEASPOON CRUSHED DRIED CHILLI

½–1 TEASPOON DRIED OREGANO

1 SMALL WATERMELON

150G FETA, CRUMBLED

4 SPRING ONIONS, SLICED

4 TABLESPOONS FRUITY EXTRA VIRGIN OLIVE OIL

A GOOD HANDFUL OF GREEK BASIL OR MINT LEAVES

SALT AND FRESHLY GROUND BLACK PEPPER

Equipment

BARBECUE OR RIDGED GRIDDLE PAN

Start by marinating the prawns. Tip the prawns into a large glass or ceramic bowl and add the juice and finely grated zest of 1 lemon, garlic, crushed chilli, oregano and a good seasoning of salt and black pepper. Mix well, cover and leave to marinate in the fridge for a couple of hours.

While the prawns are marinating, cut the watermelon into chunks or slices and remove the skin. Arrange on a large platter, cover and chill in the fridge.

Preheat a barbecue or ridged griddle pan on the hob over a medium–high heat. Cook the prawns for 1–2 minutes on each side until cooked through and nicely charred. Arrange the prawns over the chilled watermelon and scatter with the feta and spring onions. Glug the olive oil over the whole dish, top with a flourish of Greek basil or mint and serve with extra lemon to squeeze over.

Melon Sangria

You could add a dash of brandy or Cointreau to this refreshing summer punch if you want to pep it up somewhat.

½ CHARENTAIS OR CANTALOUPE MELON

½ HONEYDEW MELON

1 CRISP EATING APPLE

A GOOD HANDFUL OF SEEDLESS GREEN GRAPES

75CL BOTTLE DRY WHITE WINE

½ CUCUMBER

500ML SPARKLING WHITE WINE, SODA WATER OR CLOUDY LEMONADE

ICE, TO SERVE

Peel, deseed and finely slice the melons, then tip into a large jug. Quarter, core and slice the apple, cut the grapes in half and add to the melons. Pour over the white wine and mix to combine. Cover and chill in the fridge for a couple of hours.

Cut the cucumber into thin slices and add to the jug with the sparkling wine, soda water or lemonade. Add plenty of ice and pour into tall glasses to serve.

Watermelon Margarita

I have to thank my boyfriend Hugh for this recipe and for undertaking the not-so-onerous task of coming up with what he thinks is the correct balance of juice to tequila. You may need to adjust and tweak the sugar and lime according to the sweetness of your watermelon.

SERVES 4

½ SMALL WATERMELON

4 TEASPOONS CASTER SUGAR, PLUS EXTRA IF NEEDED, TO TASTE

150ML GOLD TEQUILA

JUICE OF 2 LIMES, PLUS EXTRA IF NEEDED, TO TASTE AND TO SERVE

To serve

COARSELY GROUND SEA SALT, FOR THE GLASSES

ICE CUBES OR CRUSHED ICE

SMALL LIME WEDGES

Cut the watermelon into wedges, remove the skin and any seeds and whizz the flesh with the sugar in a blender or using a stick blender until smooth. Pour 500ml juice into a jug, add the tequila and lime juice and mix well. Taste and add more sugar and lime juice accordingly.

Spinkle a layer of salt onto a side plate. Rub the rim of each glass with a little lime juice and dip into the salt to coat. Fill the glasses with ice cubes or crushed ice, pour over the watermelon mixture and serve immediately with a small lime wedge on the side.

Melon and Papaya Salad with Lemongrass and Ginger Syrup

This vibrant, cooling and colourful fruit salad makes the most of the variety of melons that are in season at the height of summer. I would suggest using a mixture of Charentais, honeydew and Galia for a good range of flavours and colours.

SERVES 6

100G CASTER SUGAR

1 LEMONGRASS STALK, TRIMMED

2 LIME LEAVES

JUICE OF 1 LIME

5CM PIECE OF FRESH GINGER, SLICED

3 MIXED MELONS

1 RIPE PAPAYA

½ FRESH COCONUT

A HANDFUL OF REGULAR OR PINEAPPLE MINT
LEAVES, ROUGHLY CHOPPED

Start by making the syrup, as it will need to infuse and cool before adding to the melons. Tip the sugar into a small saucepan and add 100ml water. Bruise the lemongrass stalk by bashing it with the flat blade of a large knife so that it breaks and tears slightly but still holds together. Add to the pan with the lime leaves, lime juice and ginger. Place over a low heat to slowly dissolve the sugar, then bring to the boil. Simmer for 1 minute before removing from the heat and leaving until cold.

Cut the melons in half and scoop out the seeds using a spoon. Cut one half of each melon into wedges, cut away the skin and arrange on a serving plate. Cut the remaining melon into bite-sized pieces or shape into balls using a melon baller. Scatter the melon pieces or balls over the wedges. Cut the papaya in half, scoop out the seeds and remove the skin, then cut the fruit into thin slices. Scatter over the melon.

Crack the coconut, drain the coconut water into a glass and save as a cook's perk to enjoy later. Scoop out the coconut flesh and pare into thin strips using a vegetable peeler.

Strain the syrup over the melon and leave to infuse for 30 minutes. Then scatter with the coconut and mint to serve.

To check a melon for ripeness, pick it up in your hands – it should feel heavy and the underside will smell deeply fragrant if it's ripe and ready to eat.

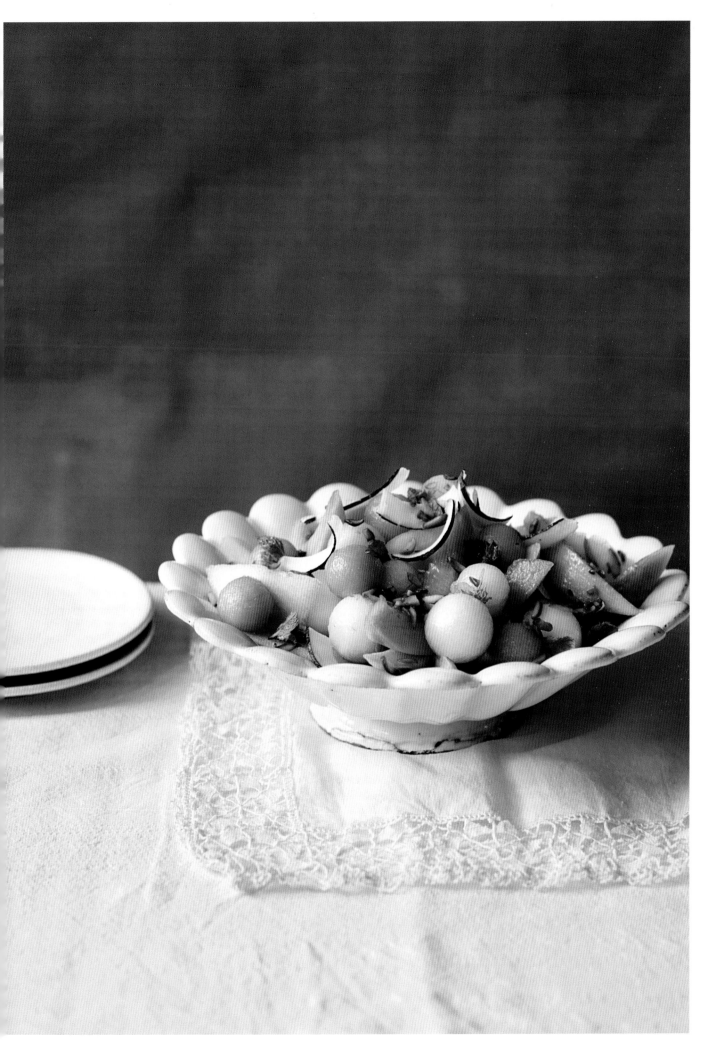

Fish Tacos with Persimmon Salsa

I first tasted fish tacos on the beach in the Hamptons after a long, strenuous day sunbathing and watching the surfers. They were served with a classic pico de gallo salsa of tomatoes, onions and chilli, but here I've added diced sweet persimmon and avocado. Have all of the elements prepared and ready to assemble before you start frying the fish and prawns – tacos should be eaten immediately after making to fully enjoy the crispy fried fish.

SERVES 4–6

1 GARLIC CLOVE, CRUSHED

8 TABLESPOONS MAYONNAISE

2 TABLESPOONS CHIPOTLE PASTE

½ SMALL WHITE CABBAGE, VERY FINELY SHREDDED

1 LITRE SUNFLOWER OIL

500G SOLE OR SNAPPER FILLETS

16 RAW LARGE SHELLED PRAWNS

6 SOFT CORN TORTILLAS

SALT AND FRESHLY GROUND BLACK PEPPER

For the persimmon salsa

1 LARGE RIPE PERSIMMON

2 TOMATOES, DICED

1 RIPE AVOCADO, DICED

1 RED CHILLI, DESEEDED AND FINELY DICED

3 SPRING ONIONS, SLICED

2 TABLESPOONS CHOPPED CORIANDER

JUICE OF 1 LIME, PLUS EXTRA LIMES TO SERVE

For the batter

125G PLAIN FLOUR

25G CORNFLOUR OR FINE POLENTA

1 TEASPOON BAKING POWDER

½ TEASPOON CAYENNE PEPPER

½ TEASPOON ANCHO OR MEDIUM CHILLI POWDER

A GOOD PINCH OF GROUND ALLSPICE

½ TEASPOON DRIED OREGANO

250–300ML COLD BEER OR SPARKLING MINERAL WATER

Equipment

SUGAR THERMOMETER

RIDGED GRIDDLE PAN (OPTIONAL)

Start by preparing the salsa. Using a vegetable peeler, remove the skin from the persimmon, then dice the flesh and tip into a bowl. Add the tomatoes, avocado, chilli, spring onions, coriander and lime juice, season with salt and black pepper and set aside.

In a small bowl, mix the garlic with 6 tablespoons of the mayonnaise and the chipotle paste, season and set aside. In a medium bowl, mix the cabbage with the remaining 2 tablespoons mayonnaise, season and set aside.

Pour the sunflower oil into a large pan, wok or deep-fat fryer, pop in a thermometer and heat the oil to 180–190°C. Cover a baking tray with a triple thickness of kitchen paper. Preheat the oven to 150°C/ gas mark 2.

When the oil has almost come up to temperature, prepare the batter. Sift the flour, cornflour or polenta, baking powder and spices into a large mixing bowl and add the oregano and a really good seasoning of salt and black pepper. Make a well in the middle of the dry ingredients and add the cold beer or sparkling water. Using a balloon whisk, very gently combine the batter – it should still be quite lumpy and most definitely not smooth, adding a little more liquid if it appears too thick. Dip the fish fillets and prawns one at a time into the batter to completely coat, allowing any excess batter to drip back into the bowl, and cook in the hot oil in batches (to avoid overcrowding and cooling the oil) for 1–2 minutes until crisp and golden. Using a slotted spoon, remove from the oil and drain on the kitchen paper- covered tray. Keep warm in the oven while you cook the remaining batches.

Warm the tortillas either on a hot ridged griddle pan over a medium heat for about 30 seconds each side, or wrapped in foil in the oven for about 10 minutes. Pile the warm tortillas with a spoonful of the cabbage coleslaw, fish fillets, prawns and salsa and serve the chipotle mayo and limes alongside.

Persimmon and Ginger Spiced Cookies

Look out for really ripe, sweet persimmons for this recipe and use fruits that are roughly the size of an apple to yield the correct amount of purée.

MAKES ABOUT 30

2 LARGE RIPE PERSIMMONS

100ML SUNFLOWER OIL

100G DARK TREACLE OR MOLASSES

300G PLAIN FLOUR

125G CASTER SUGAR

1 TEASPOON BAKING POWDER

1 TEASPOON BICARBONATE OF SODA

1½ TEASPOONS GROUND GINGER

½ TEASPOON GROUND CINNAMON

A GOOD GRATING OF NUTMEG

A PINCH OF SALT

150G GRANULATED SUGAR, FOR ROLLING

Using a small sharp knife remove the skin from the persimmons and whizz the flesh in a mini blender until almost smooth. Scoop the pulp into a small pan and set over a low heat. Stir constantly with a rubber spatula to prevent the purée scorching on the bottom of the pan and cook until the purée has reduced by half to about 140g.

Remove from the heat, tip into a bowl and add the sunflower oil and treacle or molasses and mix until smooth and leave to cool for 2-3 minutes.

Sift the flour, caster sugar, baking powder, bicarbonate of soda, spices and salt into large bowl and make a well in the centre. Add the persimmoms mixture and beat until smooth.

Preheat the oven to 180°C/gas mark 4 and line two baking trays with baking parchment.

Tip the granulated sugar onto a tray. Using your hands, roll the cookie dough into walnut-sized balls and roll each one in the granulated sugar until coated. Arrange 12 cookies on each baking tray and flatten each one slightly with your fingers. Bake on the middle shelf of the oven for 10-12 minutes until crisp but still slightly soft in the middle. Repeat with the remaining cookie dough.

Leave to cool on the trays for 1 minute and then transfer to a wire rack until cold.

Orchard

As the summer months draw to a close and berries, soft fruit and juicy peaches start to seem a distant memory, fruit lovers like myself can take heart in the promise of an early autumn harvest of apples, pears and quinces. If you are lucky enough to have an apple tree or two in your garden, then you will be all too aware of the wonderful sight of them in full blossom in the springtime, and with that – weather depending – comes the promise of a good haul of fruit later in the year.

Over the last few years there has been a renewed interest in heritage orchard fruits, and the days of surviving on only Granny Smiths, Golden Delicious and Conference pears are long gone. Us cooks are now blessed with apples in a huge range of sizes, sweetness and colour, and with over 2,000 varieties available we are spoilt for choice. The diversity of pears grown worldwide is also vast nowadays, encompassing more than 500 varieties. Given the enormity of the subject, this chapter can only scratch the surface of what could easily have been a book in itself.

Apples provide us with surely the most loved autumn pudding of all – the humble apple pie. In its purest form of apples baked in a pastry crust, it is utterly delicious and has graced more Sunday lunch tables than we can ever imagine. But the apple is worthy of so much more than a simple pie, from the French chausson and tarte Tatin through to tray bakes, cakes and even tangy caramels. If you have more than one apple tree, it's more than likely that in a good year you will have been forced to turn a bumper crop and mountains of windfalls into chutney or relish, and here you'll find a fiery, smoked chilli update on the preserve theme that is perfect for cold cuts and cheese. I myself have an apple press on my wish list so that we can turn our own apples into juice and cider next autumn.

Until relatively recently, the nearest most people got to quince was in the form of membrillo – an amber-coloured paste usually served with cheese and hailing (in slightly various forms and with different names) from the Middle East and all across southern Europe, including Spain, France, Portugal and Italy. The beautiful, ancient quince, with its slightly knobbly pear shape and glowing yellow skin that is often covered in a downy jacket, is a well-travelled fruit. It grows in Britain and throughout the Mediterranean but also as far afield as Iran, China and Argentina, and can trace its origins to Ancient Greece and Rome. Traditionally regarded as a symbol of love and fertility, some believe that it was actually a quince that was given to Adam by Eve in the Garden of Eden.

The quince in its raw form is not only beautiful, but left in a bowl will perfume a whole room with a sweet aroma. Somewhat unpalatable raw due to its highly acidic character, once cooked, the quince flesh turns almost deep red in colour and can be used in both sweet and savoury cooking. Try adding a few slices to a spiced tagine-style stew. Or grate the fruit into a preserving jar and top up with either vodka or brandy, then leave to steep for several months, shaking the jar at regular intervals, and open and enjoy come Christmas time.

Apple and Smoked Trout Salad with Cobnuts and Celery

I like salads with a bit of snap and crunch, especially if they are being served as a main course, and I also like a splash of colour and a zippy dressing. This salad meets all those criteria but needs to be made with sparkly fresh veggies – those that have been lurking in the back of the fridge simply will not do. Look out for fresh cobnuts and British Fenland celery from Cambridgeshire, along with apples and beetroots, as they are all in season at the same time. For best results, you'll need a mandolin slicer for the preparation of this salad, but if you don't have one, a sharp knife will suffice.

SERVES 4

A HANDFUL OF COBNUTS OR HAZELNUTS

1 MEDIUM PINK OR CANDY-STRIPED
BEETROOT

¼ CUCUMBER

2 CRISP SHARP APPLES, SUCH AS
GRANNY SMITH

6 RADISHES

2 CELERY STICKS

250G SMOKED TROUT FILLETS

JUICE OF ½ LEMON

5 TABLESPOONS EXTRA VIRGIN OLIVE OIL

1 TEASPOON GRAINY DIJON MUSTARD

3 TABLESPOONS SALAD CRESS

SALT AND FRESHLY GROUND BLACK PEPPER

Crack open the nut shells, pick out the nuts and roughly chop.

Peel the beetroot and slice wafer thinly, using a mandolin if you can, followed by the cucumber. Quarter and core the apples, then slice in the same way. Slice the radishes into thin discs, and cut the celery into fine matchsticks.

Arrange the veggies and apples on serving plates and flake the smoked trout alongside or over the top.

In a small bowl, lightly whisk together the lemon juice, olive oil and mustard, then season well with salt and black pepper. Drizzle the dressing over the salads, scatter with the salad cress and serve.

Slow-roasted Pork with Spiced Apple Relish and Cider Gravy

A great roast pork joint with salty, super-crunchy crackling is not only a thing of beauty but a spectacularly good crowd pleaser, whether it be for Sunday lunch or served around a bonfire shredded into crusty bread rolls with a drizzle of the warm pan juices, a handful of rocket and a good helping of the apple relish. More often than not you'll be fighting hands away from the meat as you're carving. Pay a visit to your local friendly butcher for a really good cut of meat that has been well prepared and comes from a pig that has been reared with care and attention. Apples feature three ways in this dish: apple relish that is cooked in the oven alongside the meat, in stuffing balls and as a rich cider gravy.

SERVES 6–8

For the pork

2 TEASPOONS FENNEL SEEDS

1 TEASPOON CORIANDER SEEDS

1 TEASPOON BLACK PEPPERCORNS

1 TEASPOON CRUSHED DRIED CHILLI

½ TEASPOON DRIED OREGANO

3 TEASPOONS SEA SALT FLAKES, PLUS EXTRA

4 GARLIC CLOVES, CRUSHED

FINELY GRATED ZEST OF 1 UNWAXED LEMON

3KG BONE-IN LOIN OF PORK, CHINED AND SKIN DEEPLY SCORED

1–2 TABLESPOONS OLIVE OIL

FRESHLY GROUND BLACK PEPPER

For the stuffing

1 ONION, FINELY CHOPPED

1 FAT GARLIC CLOVE, CRUSHED

1 CRISP EATING APPLE, PEELED, CORED AND COARSELY GRATED

10 SAGE LEAVES, FINELY CHOPPED

½ TEASPOON FENNEL SEEDS

400G GOOD-QUALITY SAUSAGE MEAT

100G FRESH WHITE BREADCRUMBS

40G SLICED PANCETTA, FINELY CHOPPED

SALT AND FRESHLY GROUND BLACK PEPPER

For the relish and gravy

2 COOKING APPLES, PEELED, QUARTERED AND CORED

50G UNSALTED BUTTER

1 ROUNDED TABLESPOON GOLDEN CASTER SUGAR

1 CINNAMON STICK

A PINCH OF CRUSHED DRIED CHILLI

A GRATING OF NUTMEG

500ML DRY CIDER

1 TABLESPOON PLAIN FLOUR

SALT AND FRESHLY GROUND BLACK PEPPER

Preheat the oven to 220°C/gas mark 7.

Get the pork ready for the oven first. Using a pestle and mortar, lightly crush the fennel and coriander seeds and black peppercorns. Add the chilli, oregano, salt, garlic and lemon zest and mix to a paste. Push the mixture into the slits in the pork skin using your fingers. Place the pork, skin-side uppermost, in a roasting tin and rub the skin with the olive oil. Season well with sea salt flakes and black pepper and roast on the middle shelf of the oven for 20–25 minutes until the skin starts to crisp.

Meanwhile, prepare the stuffing. Cook the onion in a tablespoon of olive oil in a frying pan until soft but not coloured. Add the garlic, cook for another minute, then tip into a bowl and leave to cool slightly. Add the remaining ingredients, season well and, using clean hands, combine thoroughly. Roll the mixture into 12–16 balls, arrange on a baking tray, cover with clingfilm and chill for 30 minutes.

Turn the oven down to 170°C/gas mark 3 and cook the pork for a further 2 hours.

Meanwhile, prepare the relish. Place the apple quarters in a small roasting tin, dot each with a knob of the butter, sprinkle with the sugar, add the cinnamon stick, chilli and nutmeg and splash over 3 tablespoons of the cider. Cover with foil and cook in the oven for about 25 minutes until the apples are tender and have reduced to a thick pulp. Remove from the oven, taste and add a little more sugar if needed.

Turn the oven up to 220°C/gas mark 7, add the stuffing balls to the oven and continue to cook the pork for a further 20–25 minutes until the skin is very crisp and the stuffing balls are golden brown. Transfer the pork and stuffing to a serving dish, cover with foil and leave to

rest for 15 minutes. Spoon off all but 1 tablespoon of the fat from the tin and place over a gentle heat. Stir in the flour, cook for 30 seconds, then add the remaining cider. Bring to the boil, stirring constantly and incorporating any bits from the base of the tin. Taste and season with salt and black pepper, and perhaps a little sugar to balance the acidity from the cider.

Slice the pork and serve with the apple relish, stuffing and cider gravy. And don't forget the crackling.

Gingerbread Spiced Apple Doughnuts

These delicately spiced doughnuts are filled with tart apple purée and coated in either sugar or a lip-smacking lemon glaze. I make them slightly smaller than normal so that eating two (or three) in one sitting doesn't seem at all greedy.

MAKES ABOUT 16 SMALLISH DOUGHNUTS

For the filling

1 BRAMLEY APPLE, PEELED AND ROUGHLY CHOPPED

3 SMALL EATING APPLES, PEELED AND ROUGHLY CHOPPED

JUICE OF ½ LEMON

2 TABLESPOONS CASTER SUGAR

15G UNSALTED BUTTER

For the doughnuts

175ML FULL-FAT MILK

50G LIGHT MUSCOVADO SUGAR

10G ACTIVE DRIED YEAST (NOT FAST-ACTION/EASY-BLEND)

450G STRONG WHITE FLOUR, PLUS EXTRA FOR DUSTING

1 TEASPOON GROUND CINNAMON

½ TEASPOON GROUND GINGER

A GENEROUS PINCH OF GROUND CLOVES

A GOOD GRATING OF NUTMEG

½ TEASPOON SEA SALT

1 LARGE EGG, BEATEN

1 LARGE EGG YOLK

1 ROUNDED TABLESPOON DARK TREACLE OR MOLASSES

75G UNSALTED BUTTER, SOFTENED

1.5 LITRES SUNFLOWER OR GROUNDNUT OIL

125G CASTER SUGAR

JUICE OF ½ LEMON

3–5 TABLESPOONS ICING SUGAR

Equipment

6CM PLAIN COOKIE CUTTER

SUGAR THERMOMETER

LARGE PIPING BAG FITTED WITH A 1CM PLAIN NOZZLE

Put all the filling ingredients into a large saucepan, half cover and cook over a low–medium heat, stirring frequently, for 5–6 minutes until the apples become a soft pulp. Uncover and continue to cook, stirring frequently, until thickened. Remove from the heat and leave until cold.

To make the doughnuts, heat the milk until warm to the touch, add 1 teaspoon of the muscovado sugar and the yeast and whisk to combine. Leave in a warm place for about 5 minutes until a thick foam has formed on top of the milk.

Tip the flour, remaining muscovado sugar, spices and salt into the bowl of a free-standing mixer fitted with the dough hook. Make a well in the centre and add the yeasty milk, whole egg, egg yolk, treacle or molasses and butter. Mix steadily for about 5 minutes until the dough is smooth and elastic – it will still be slightly sticky. Shape into a smooth ball and place in a large, lightly oiled mixing bowl. Cover with clingfilm and leave to prove in a warm, draught-free place for at least 1 hour or until the dough has doubled in size.

Tip onto a work surface and knead gently for 30 seconds to knock out any air bubbles. Lightly dust the work surface with flour and roll the dough out to a thickness of 1.5–2cm. Using the cutter, stamp out discs and arrange on two lightly floured baking trays, leaving plenty of space between each one. Cover loosely with oiled clingfilm and leave to rise again for 30–45 minutes.

Pour the oil into a large saucepan so that it comes at least 10cm up the sides and heat to 180–190°C. Cover a large baking tray with a triple thickness of kitchen paper and tip the caster sugar into a large bowl. In a small bowl, mix the lemon juice and icing sugar until smooth.

Fry the doughnuts in batches – 4 at most – for about 2 minutes on each side or until deep golden brown. Remove and drain thoroughly on the kitchen paper before either tossing in the caster sugar or brushing with the lemon glaze. Make sure the oil returns to temperature before frying the next batch. Cool on a wire rack.

Make a small incision in the side of each doughnut. Fill the piping bag with the apple mixture and pipe through the incision into the middle of each doughnut.

Apple Chaussons

The success of this recipe requires you to make puff pastry, but please stop for a moment before you turn the page or add ready-made puff pastry to your shopping list. It's really not tricky and the results more than make up for the small amount of effort and skill involved – once you've tasted the difference that homemade flaky, buttery pastry makes, you'll be convinced. Use firm, crisp eating apples for the filling, as they will retain some texture during baking.

MAKES 14–16

For the puff pastry

150G PLAIN FLOUR, PLUS EXTRA FOR DUSTING

100G STRONG WHITE FLOUR

A PINCH OF SEA SALT

250G UNSALTED BUTTER, CHILLED

1 MEDIUM EGG YOLK, LIGHTLY BEATEN

100ML ICED WATER

1 TEASPOON LEMON JUICE

1 MEDIUM EGG, BEATEN, TO GLAZE

For the filling

4 EATING APPLES, SUCH AS BRAEBURN OR GOLDEN DELICIOUS, PEELED AND THINLY SLICED

15G UNSALTED BUTTER

2 TABLESPOONS GOLDEN CASTER SUGAR

1 TABLESPOON LEMON JUICE

Equipment

12CM FLUTED COOKIE CUTTER

For the pastry, combine the flours and salt in a mixing bowl, add 50g chilled diced butter and rub in using your fingertips. Make a well in the centre and add the egg yolk. Mix the iced water with the lemon juice and add 75ml, mixing with a round-bladed knife to bring the dough together – you may need to add a drop more liquid but the dough shouldn't be too wet. Gather into a ball and flatten into a rectangle. Cover with clingfilm and chill for 1 hour.

Lightly dust the work surface with flour. Roll the dough into a rectangle three times as long as it is wide (15 x 45cm), with one of the shortest sides nearest to you. Place the remaining 200g butter between two sheets of baking parchment and, using a rolling pin, flatten it

into a neat square slightly smaller than one-third of the pastry rectangle. Place the butter on the middle section of pastry, fold the bottom third up over it, brush off the excess flour and fold the top third down so that the butter is encased. Brush off any excess flour and turn the square 90 degrees clockwise. Roll into a similar-sized rectangle as before, trying to keep it as neat as possible, then again fold the bottom third up over the middle third and the top third down, brushing off excess flour each time. Lightly press the pastry edges together, turn 90 degrees clockwise, wrap in clingfilm and chill for 1 hour.

Repeat this rolling, folding and turning twice more so that you have rolled it 5 times in total. Leave in the fridge for 2 hours before using.

Meanwhile, tip the apples into a saucepan with the butter and sugar. Cover and cook over a gentle heat for about 5 minutes until soft and tender but not mushy, stirring to prevent the apples catching on the base of the pan. Add the lemon juice and leave to cool.

Roll out the pastry on a lightly floured work surface to a thickness of 2mm and, using the cutter, stamp out discs. Spoon a tablespoonful of filling into a mound onto one half of each disc. Brush the other half with a little cold water, fold over the filling and press the edges together to seal. Using a small knife, knock up the edges, brush the pastry with the beaten egg and arrange on baking parchment-covered baking trays. Chill for 30 minutes.

Preheat the oven to 190°C/gas mark 5. Brush the pastries again with eggwash and, using the point of a small sharp knife, score a leaf pattern into the pastry, being careful not to cut all the way through. Bake on the middle shelf for 20–25 minutes until well risen and golden brown. Serve warm or at room temperature.

Apple Tarte Tatin

I had not intended to include an apple pie as such in this book, my thinking being that the world did not need another recipe for such a classic. But when I got to thinking about my favourite apple pie – both to make and eat – tarte Tatin was top of the list. It's traditionally made with either puff pastry or a rich shortcrust, but I've come up with what I think is a far better option. This cream cheese pastry is not only just about the easiest pastry to make, it's utterly delicious. The quantities of butter and cream cheese might look excessive, but trust me. This is one helluva pastry that is more than capable of standing up to the punch of the caramelised apples.

SERVES 6

For the cream cheese pastry
200G PLAIN FLOUR, PLUS EXTRA FOR DUSTING

A PINCH OF SEA SALT

200G UNSALTED BUTTER, CHILLED AND DICED

180G FULL-FAT CREAM CHEESE

For the top
75G UNSALTED BUTTER, AT ROOM TEMPERATURE

75G CASTER SUGAR

6–8 FIRM EATING APPLES, SUCH AS COX'S, BRAEBURN, SPARTAN OR GOLDEN DELICIOUS, PEELED, CORED AND QUARTERED

CRÈME FRAÎCHE, TO SERVE

Equipment
26CM CAST-IRON OR OVENPROOF FRYING PAN

30–35CM PLATE OR PAN, AS A GUIDE FOR CUTTING

To make the pastry, tip the flour and salt into the bowl of a food processor, add the butter and pulse for 5 seconds – just long enough to cover the butter pieces in flour. Add the cream cheese in teaspoonfuls and pulse again until the butter and cream cheese have nearly been rubbed into the flour – you still want to see flecks of both.

Tip out onto a lightly floured work surface and lightly knead to bring the dough into a slightly raggedy ball. Flatten into a fat disc, cover with clingfilm and chill for at least 2 hours.

Preheat the oven to 190°C/gas mark 5. Smear the butter evenly over the base and sides of the frying pan, sprinkle with the sugar, then arrange the apple quarters in tight concentric circles, core-side uppermost, on top. Set the pan over a medium heat and cook the apples without stirring or moving them for 8–10 minutes until the butter and sugar have melted and started to caramelise. Check by carefully lifting one apple quarter and peeking at the underside – it should be tinged with golden brown caramel. Remove from the heat.

Lightly dust the work surface with flour. Roll out the pastry and, using the plate or pan guide, cut into a 30–35cm disc, then trim the edges to neaten. Carefully lift and place the pastry over the apples, then using a palette knife, carefully push the edges down into the pan around the inside rim so that they are encased in a pastry pillow. Return the pan to a medium heat for 1 minute so that the pastry just starts to seal and cook around the edges, then slide onto the middle shelf of the oven and bake for 25–30 minutes until the pastry is golden brown, crisp and flaky.

Leave to cool in the pan for 2 minutes, then run a palette knife around the edge to loosen. Place a serving plate on top of the pan and, holding the pan and plate firmly in an oven cloth, flip over so that the tart turns out onto the plate. Serve immediately with crème fraîche.

Apple Caramels

If you are lucky enough to have an apple tree or two, you will be all too aware of the inevitable glut that a good harvest brings. Here's a way to use up a number of apples when you have tired of apple pies and juicing.

MAKES 30–40

1 LITRE CLOUDY UNPASTEURISED OR FRESHLY SQUEEZED AND FILTERED APPLE JUICE

1 CINNAMON STICK

1–2 STAR ANISE

2 CLOVES

75G UNSALTED BUTTER, DICED, PLUS EXTRA FOR GREASING

175G LIGHT MUSCOVADO SUGAR

125G CASTER SUGAR

125G CRÈME FRAÎCHE

A GOOD PINCH OF SEA SALT FLAKES

Equipment

18CM SQUARE BAKING TIN OR EQUIVALENT-SIZED RECTANGULAR TIN

SUGAR THERMOMETER

Grease and line the baking tin with baking parchment.

To make the apple caramel syrup, pour the apple juice into a large saucepan, add the whole spices and bring to the boil. Cook steadily over a low–medium heat until the juice has reduced to 125g of honey-coloured syrup. Pick the spices out of the syrup before weighing to get an accurate measure, and note that it is easier to do this by weight rather than measure it by volume in a jug.

Pour the syrup into a clean 2-litre saucepan and add the butter, both sugars and the crème fraîche. Set the pan over a low heat and stir frequently to melt the butter and dissolve the sugar. Add the thermometer to the pan, bring to the boil and cook at a steady, even pace, stirring from time to time, until the syrup reaches 126°C. Slide the pan off the heat, then remove the thermometer, add the sea salt flakes and stir to combine with a rubber spatula.

Pour the syrup into the prepared tin and leave until completely cold before cutting into squares with a lightly greased knife and wrapping in twists of waxed paper or baking parchment. To make cutting easier, pop the caramel into the fridge for 1 hour to firm up. The caramels will keep for up to 1 week in an airtight box in the fridge.

To make the juice for the syrup, you can press the apples through a juicer and then filter through coffee filter papers, or use a fresh cloudy unpasteurised apple juice like those available from fruit farms. The reduced apple syrup is not only delicious in these caramels, but if you stop cooking the juice when it reaches 175–200g, it makes a wonderful syrup to pour over cakes and pancakes, or try the Apple Caramel Crumb Bars on page 212.

Apple Caramel Crumb Bars

Everyone needs a recipe for apple crumble in their repertoire. It's also useful to be able to rustle up a fruity tray bake for portable snacks or weekend teas. These bars tick all of those boxes and more besides. The apple caramel syrup really gives them a boost, but if you're not inclined to make it, you could substitute maple syrup at a pinch.

MAKES 12–16 BARS

200G PLAIN FLOUR

50G WHOLEGRAIN SPELT FLOUR

125G GOLDEN CASTER SUGAR

½ TEASPOON BAKING POWDER

A PINCH OF SEA SALT

175G UNSALTED BUTTER, CHILLED AND DICED, PLUS EXTRA FOR GREASING

100G ROLLED OATS

1 MEDIUM EGG YOLK

2 TABLESPOONS DOUBLE CREAM OR FULL-FAT MILK

75G WALNUTS, ROUGHLY CHOPPED

3 TABLESPOONS APPLE CARAMEL SYRUP (SEE PAGE 211) OR MAPLE SYRUP

For the filling

6 CRISP EATING APPLES

JUICE OF ½ LEMON

½ TEASPOON GROUND CINNAMON

125ML APPLE JUICE

A PINCH OF SEA SALT

2 TEASPOONS CORNFLOUR

Equipment

20 x 30CM BAKING TIN, 4CM DEEP

Start by making the filling. Peel, core and slice the apples directly into a large saucepan, then add the lemon juice, cinnamon, half the apple juice and the salt. Half cover and cook over a medium heat for about 5 minutes until the slices are just tender but not mushy. In a small bowl, whisk together the cornflour with the remaining apple juice. Add to the pan, stir well and cook for 45 seconds–1 minute until the mixture has thickened and the cornflour has been cooked out. Slide the pan off the heat and leave the apples to cool to room temperature while you prepare the base and topping.

Grease the baking tin and line the base and sides with a large sheet of baking parchment. Preheat the oven to 170°C/gas mark 3.

Tip both flours into the bowl of a food processor and add the sugar, baking powder and salt. Pulse to combine and then add the butter and pulse again until it has been rubbed into the dry ingredients. Add the rolled oats and pulse until combined and the mixture starts to clump together. Tip into a large mixing bowl. Mix the egg yolk with the cream or milk and add to the crumble mix. Stir together using a palette knife and then your fingers until combined. Spoon three-quarters of the crumble mix into the prepared tin and press into an even layer with your hands to form the base. Bake on the middle shelf of the oven for about 15 minutes until pale golden brown.

Mix the walnuts into the remaining crumble. Spoon the apple filling onto the base in an even layer, drizzle over the syrup and scatter with the walnut crumble. Bake on the middle shelf of the oven for about 30 minutes or until the crumble is golden brown and the apples are bubbling. Leave to cool completely and then cut into bars to serve.

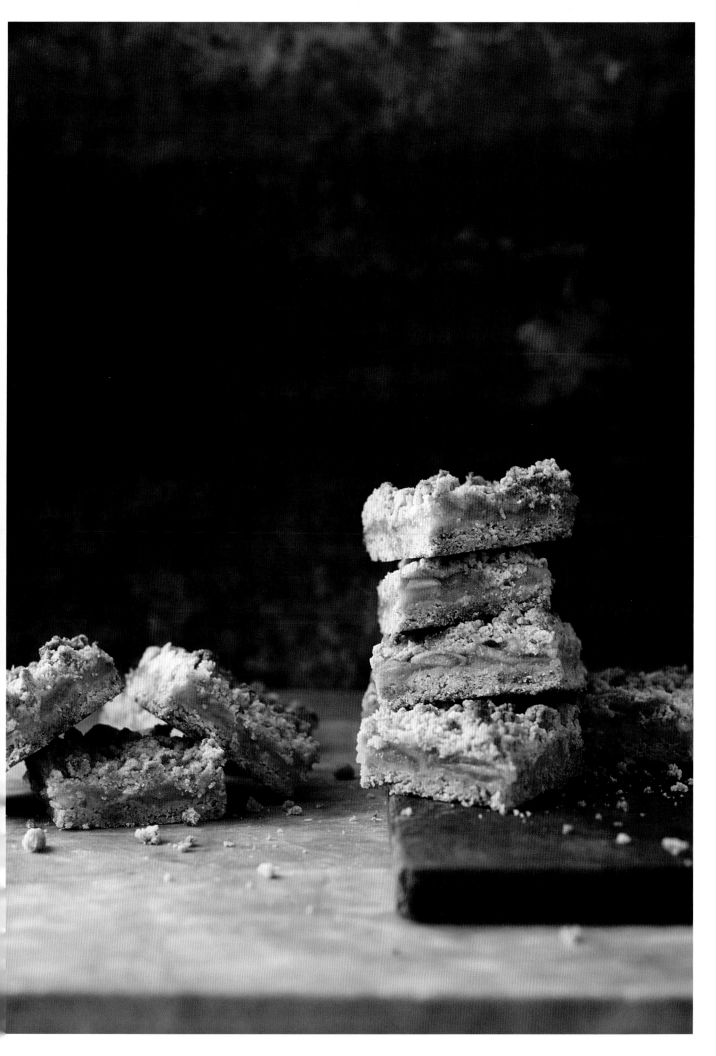

Smoky Apple and Pear Relish

This snappy, fruity relish is just the ticket to serve with a nutty hard cheese or cold cuts. When cooking preserves and pickles, I tend to make smaller batches, as I find it easier and more accurate to double the quantities if I have a glut of fruit rather than having to reduce quantities to make a small number of jars. This also means that I can fill my cupboards with a nice variety of preserves rather than having groaning shelves of a single type.

MAKES 4 JARS

2 LARGE DRIED SMOKED CHIPOTLE CHILLIES

4 CRISP EATING APPLES, PEELED AND DICED

4 FIRM PEARS, PEELED AND DICED

400ML CIDER VINEGAR

325G LIGHT MUSCOVADO SUGAR

3 LARGE SHALLOTS, FINELY CHOPPED

2 GARLIC CLOVES, CRUSHED

4CM PIECE OF FRESH GINGER, GRATED

1 TEASPOON FENNEL SEEDS

1 TEASPOON CAYENNE PEPPER

½ TEASPOON FRESHLY GROUND
BLACK PEPPER

1 TEASPOON SEA SALT FLAKES

Equipment
4 x 450G JAM JARS

Soak the chipotle chillies in a bowl of just-boiled water while you prepare the remaining ingredients.

Tip the fruit into a large stainless steel saucepan and add all the other ingredients. Drain the chipotle chillies, remove the stalks and finely chop the chillies, seeds and all. Add to the pan and stir to combine. Set over a low–medium heat and slowly bring to the boil, stirring from time to time. Continue to cook over a low–medium heat for about 40 minutes or until the fruit is very tender and the liquid is reduced, thickened and syrupy.

Slide the pan off the heat and spoon the chutney into the warm sterilised jars (see page 132). Seal with the lids and leave until cold before labelling. Store in a cool, dark cupboard for 1 month before opening, then store in the fridge and use within 2 months. The unopened chutney will keep for up to 6 months.

Homemade Yogurt with Honey-baked Apples and Pears and Granola

Clearly, it's not strictly necessary to make your own yogurt, but if you're anything like me then you'll get enormous satisfaction from sitting down to eat breakfast knowing that you've cooked all the elements from scratch. The yoghurt and granola in this recipe will most likely make more than you need in one sitting but both will provide you with delicious homemade breakfasts for a week.

SERVES 6

For the yogurt

1 LITRE FULL-FAT ORGANIC MILK

75G ORGANIC NATURAL LIVE YOGURT

For the granola

100G ROLLED OATS

50G RYE OR SPELT FLAKES

50G WHOLE OR FLAKED ALMONDS

50G SHELLED UNSALTED PISTACHIOS

75G MIXED SEEDS, SUCH AS PUMPKIN, SESAME AND LINSEED

100G CLEAR HONEY

2 TABLESPOONS OLIVE OIL

1 TEASPOON VANILLA EXTRACT OR BEAN PASTE

¼ TEASPOON GROUND CINNAMON

A PINCH OF SEA SALT

For the compote

3 APPLES, QUARTERED AND CORED

2 PEARS, QUARTERED AND CORED

3 TABLESPOONS CLEAR HONEY

1 TEASPOON VANILLA BEAN PASTE

50G UNSALTED BUTTER

A GOOD PINCH OF GROUND CINNAMON

A GOOD GRATING OF NUTMEG

Equipment

SUGAR THERMOMETER

LARGE KILNER OR OTHER PRESERVING JAR

Start by making the yogurt. Pour the milk into a large saucepan, place over a low–medium heat and bring to 82°C. Immediately slide the pan off the heat, leaving in the thermometer, and allow to cool until the milk reaches 45°C. Add the yogurt and mix to combine, then pour into the warm sterilised preserving jar (see page 132). Seal with the lid, wrap the jar in a double or triple thickness of clean tea towels and leave in a warm place such as at the side of the hob or on top of the oven for at least 4 hours and up to 12 until thickened – don't stir.

To make the granola, preheat the oven to 150°C/gas mark 2 and line a large baking tray with baking parchment. Tip the oats, rye or spelt flakes, nuts and seeds into a large mixing bowl. Add the remaining granola ingredients and mix well to combine. Spoon onto the baking tray and toast in the oven for about 30 minutes until golden brown and crisp, stirring frequently to ensure that it cooks evenly. Leave to cool before scooping into a jar or airtight container.

For the compote, preheat the oven to 180°C/gas mark 4 and line a medium-sized baking tin with baking parchment. Tip in the fruit, drizzle over the honey and vanilla bean paste, dot over the butter and sprinkle with the spices. Mix gently to coat, then cook on the middle shelf for about 40 minutes until the fruit is tender and burnished with golden, buttery caramel juices. Leave to cool slightly and then serve with the yogurt and granola for a mighty fine breakfast.

Rather like making sourdough bread where you add a starter to the dough, yoghurt follows the same principle and you add live yoghurt to warm milk to create a bacteria culture. It's easy to keep an ongoing supply, simply hold back 75g from your first batch of yoghurt to make the next.
If you don't want to use your oven to ferment the yoghurt, pour it into a vacuum flask, seal and leave until cooled and thickened. Transfer into clean jars and store in the fridge until needed.

Hibiscus Poached Pears

I first cooked and tasted this dish while working with Suzanne Zeidy, an inspirational Egyptian food writer and restaurateur, and this is my variation on her recipe. Dried hibiscus flowers are available in Middle Eastern food shops or from online suppliers and impart a wonderful deep colour and slightly floral note to the pears.

SERVES 6

6 RIPE WILLIAMS OR CONFERENCE PEARS

25G DRIED HIBISCUS FLOWERS

2 STRIPS OF RIND FROM AN UNWAXED LEMON

2 STRIPS OF ORANGE RIND

200G CASTER SUGAR

300ML SWEET ROSÉ WINE

2 STAR ANISE

Peel the pears using a vegetable peeler, leaving the stalks intact.

Tip the hibiscus flowers, strips of lemon and orange rind, sugar and rosé wine into a large saucepan that will snuggly hold the pears in a single layer. Add the star anise and bring to the boil to dissolve the sugar. Carefully submerge the pears in the liquid, adding just enough water to cover them, then cover the surface of the liquid with a disc of baking parchment.

Cook the pears at a very gentle simmer for about 30 minutes or until they are tender. The cooking time will depend on the ripeness and size of the pears, so to check for doneness, push a small sharp knife into a pear. Once they are cooked, remove from the heat but leave in the liquid until completely cold or until ready to serve. The longer you leave the pears in the liquid, the deeper the red colouring from the hibiscus flowers will penetrate the fruit.

Arrange the pears in a serving dish and strain some of the poaching liquid around them to serve.

Dried hibiscus flowers are more often used to make a delicious and refreshing herbal tea. The flowers are steeped in boiling water, which is then sweetened, strained and the tea served cold over ice.

Chocolate Sablé Choux Buns with Pears and Chocolate Sauce

Chocolate and pears are a classic pairing, as are choux buns with chocolate sauce, so it makes sense to combine them all in one sweet morsel. The contrast with the caramelised pears and cream filling and the hot chocolate sauce is sublime.

MAKES 30–35 SMALL BUNS; SERVES 6

For the sablé

40G UNSALTED BUTTER, SOFTENED

50G SOFT LIGHT BROWN SUGAR

40G PLAIN FLOUR

10G COCOA POWDER

A PINCH OF GROUND CINNAMON

A PINCH OF SEA SALT

For the choux buns

100ML MILK

80G UNSALTED BUTTER, DICED

A PINCH OF SEA SALT

1 TEASPOON CASTER SUGAR

125G PLAIN FLOUR

4 MEDIUM EGGS, LIGHTLY BEATEN

For the pears and sauce

4 PEARS, PEELED AND CUT INTO SMALL DICE

75G CASTER SUGAR

600ML DOUBLE CREAM

150G DARK CHOCOLATE, CHOPPED

1 ROUNDED TABLESPOON SOFT LIGHT BROWN SUGAR

2 TABLESPOONS MARSALA

Equipment

LARGE PIPING BAG FITTED WITH A 1CM PLAIN NOZZLE

1.5CM PLAIN COOKIE CUTTER

Start by preparing the sablé. Cream together the butter and sugar. Add the flour, cocoa, cinnamon and salt and mix, then very lightly knead the dough in your hands until smooth. Flatten into a disc, place between two sheets of baking parchment and roll out to a thickness of 1–2mm. Chill for 1 hour.

For the choux buns, preheat the oven to 180°C/gas mark 4 and line two baking trays with baking parchment. Place the milk, butter, salt, sugar and 100ml cold water in a saucepan over a medium heat and stir to melt the butter. Bring to the boil, then immediately slide the pan off the heat and quickly sift in the flour. Using a wooden spoon, beat vigorously until the batter is smooth. Return to a low heat and cook, stirring constantly, for a further minute until the mixture is silky smooth and leaves the sides of the pan cleanly.

Tip into the bowl of a free-standing mixer and gradually add the eggs, mixing well until the batter is silky smooth and reluctantly drops off a spoon – you might not need all the egg. Scoop into the piping bag and pipe 30–35 small buns over the lined baking trays, leaving space between each to allow for expansion. Using the cutter, stamp out the same number of discs from the sablé dough. Place one disc on top of each bun and bake on the middle shelf for about 12 minutes until the buns are golden brown and puffed up and the sablé is crumbly. Make a hole in the side of each bun with a skewer and return to the oven for a further minute to dry out the insides. Leave to cool on a wire rack.

Tip the pears into a large frying pan, sprinkle with the caster sugar and place over a medium heat. Cook, stirring frequently, for 3–4 minutes until the pears are tender and caramelised. Leave to cool.

Whip half the cream until it holds firm peaks. Tip the remaining cream, chocolate and brown sugar into a saucepan and heat over a low heat, stirring constantly to melt the chocolate. Add the Marsala and stir until smooth. To serve, cut each choux bun in half, spoon the pears onto the bottom half and top with whipped cream and the choux lid. Serve with the warm chocolate sauce.

Crème Caramels with Marsala Baked Pears

The addition of crème fraîche makes for a richer crème caramel. Like the pears, it can be made ahead of time, but the pears should be at room temperature when served. For a less labour-intensive dessert, you could serve the pears warm with vanilla ice cream and warm chocolate sauce.

SERVES 6

For the crème caramel

200G CASTER SUGAR

350ML FULL-FAT MILK

1 VANILLA POD, SPLIT IN HALF LENGTHWAYS

4 MEDIUM EGGS

2 MEDIUM EGG YOLKS

175ML CRÈME FRAÎCHE

For the pears

6 SMALL RIPE PEARS, HALVED AND CORED USING A MELON BALLER

125G CASTER SUGAR

1 VANILLA POD, SPLIT IN HALF LENGTHWAYS, THEN CUT IN HALF AGAIN ACROSS THE MIDDLE

1 CINNAMON STICK

50G BLANCHED HAZELNUTS

250ML MARSALA

JUICE OF 1 LEMON

Equipment

6 INDIVIDUAL PUDDING BASINS OR 150ML RAMEKINS

FINE-MESH NYLON SIEVE

To make the crème caramel, heat 125g of the sugar with 2 tablespoons of hot water in a small, heavy-bottomed saucepan over a low heat and dissolve without stirring. Increase the heat slightly and continue to cook, brushing down the sides of the pan with a wet pastry brush if sugar crystals start to form. As the caramel starts to colour, gently swirl the pan to ensure that it cooks evenly. When a deep amber colour, and working quickly to prevent it overcooking, divide it between the basins or ramekins and leave until cold and hardened.

Pour the milk into the caramel pan, add the vanilla seeds and the pod and bring slowly to the boil. The moment the milk starts to boil, remove from the heat and leave to infuse for 20 minutes.

In a large bowl, whisk together the whole eggs, yolks and remaining sugar, but don't over-mix to avoid creating air bubbles. Mix in the crème fraîche. Reheat the milk over a low heat and pour into the egg mixture, whisking to combine. Strain through a fine-mesh nylon sieve into a large jug and set aside for 2 hours to allow the custard to settle and any air bubbles to disperse.

Preheat the oven to 150°C/gas mark 2. Arrange the basins or ramekins in a roasting tin and divide the custard equally between them. Slide the tin onto the middle shelf and pour boiling water into the tin so that it comes halfway up the sides of the basins or ramekins. Cook for 20–25 minutes until set with a very slight wobble in the middle. Carefully remove the crème caramels from the oven, leaving them in the bain-marie until completely cool, then cover with clingfilm and chill overnight.

Preheat the oven to 170°C/gas mark 3. Arrange the pears, cut-side uppermost, in a roasting tin and sprinkle with the sugar. Pop the vanilla pod pieces amongst the pears with the cinnamon stick and hazelnuts. Pour the Marsala, 100ml cold water and the lemon juice around the pears and bake on the middle shelf of the oven for about 25 minutes until tender. Remove from the oven and leave to cool to room temperature.

To serve, run a palette knife around the edge of each basin or ramekin to release the crème caramels and turn out onto serving plates. Arrange the baked pears alongside and serve with the caramel and pear pan juices.

Spiced Ginger and Chocolate Cake with Salted Caramel Pears

Like most gingerbread cakes, this benefits from being baked 24 hours in advance of serving to allow the spices to mature. Setting a timer helps ensure it's cooked enough to hold the weight of the pears halfway through baking.

SERVES 8

150G UNSALTED BUTTER, PLUS EXTRA FOR GREASING

100G GOLDEN SYRUP

75G DARK TREACLE

150G SOFT DARK BROWN SUGAR

50G DARK CHOCOLATE, 70% COCOA SOLIDS, CHOPPED

150ML STOUT OR BOILING WATER

2 NUGGETS OF STEM GINGER, CHOPPED

½ TEASPOON BICARBONATE OF SODA

200G PLAIN FLOUR

1 TEASPOON BAKING POWDER

3–4 TEASPOONS GROUND GINGER

1 ROUNDED TEASPOON GROUND CINNAMON

½ TEASPOON GROUND MIXED SPICE

¼ TEASPOON FRESHLY GROUND BLACK PEPPER

A PINCH OF CHILLI POWDER

A PINCH OF FINE SEA SALT

3 LARGE EGGS, BEATEN

For the pears

4 SMALL RIPE PEARS

20G UNSALTED BUTTER

1 TABLESPOON STEM GINGER SYRUP

For the sauce

100G CASTER SUGAR

300ML DOUBLE CREAM

3 TABLESPOONS BOURBON

25G DARK CHOCOLATE

A PINCH OF SEA SALT

Equipment

900G LOAF TIN, 11 x 26CM ACROSS THE TOP

Preheat the oven to 170°C/gas mark 3 and position a shelf in the bottom third of the oven. Grease the loaf tin and line the base and sides with a strip of greased baking parchment.

In a large saucepan, heat the butter, golden syrup, treacle, sugar, chocolate and stout over a low heat, stirring frequently to dissolve the sugar and melt the butter. When smooth, remove from the heat, add the stem ginger and bicarbonate of soda, then leave to cool.

Sift the flour, baking powder, spices and salt into a large mixing bowl. Whisk the eggs into the syrup mixture and add to the dry ingredients in three batches, beating really well after each addition and again for 1 minute once all the syrup mixture has been incorporated. Pour the batter into the prepared tin and bake for 30 minutes (set a timer) while you prepare the pears.

Peel, quarter and core the pears, leaving the stalk intact, and tip into a small roasting tin. Add the butter and ginger syrup (or 25g caster sugar), toss to coat and cook the pears on the shelf above the cake for 15–20 minutes until tender and starting to caramelise at the edges.

After 30 minutes, remove the cake from the oven and arrange the pears on top – the cake should have cooked enough for them not to sink into and deflate it. Bake for a further 30 minutes until well risen and a skewer inserted into the middle comes out clean. Leave to cool in the tin for 30 minutes, then transfer to a wire rack until cold.

Once the cake is cold, prepare the sauce. Place the sugar in a heavy-bottomed saucepan, add 2 tablespoons cold water and set over a low heat to dissolve the sugar without stirring. Increase the heat and continue to cook the syrup until it becomes an amber-coloured caramel. Slide the pan off the heat and slowly stir in the cream. Return to a low heat to re-melt any hardened caramel. Add the bourbon, chocolate and salt and heat until smooth and combined. Serve the cake with caramel sauce poured over.

Butternut Soup with Pears and Chestnuts

There's something comforting about a large pot of soup bubbling away on the stove. I love the sweet creaminess of butternut squash and the bright, orangey–yellow colour of this soup is enough to lift the spirits on a dank autumn afternoon. Squash or pumpkin pairs beautifully with spiced salami or chorizo, or salty smoked bacon, but add some cooked woodsy chestnuts and sweet tender pears and the combination really sings.

SERVES 6–8

1 LARGE ONION, DICED

1 SMALL LEEK, DICED

1 CELERY STICK, DICED

1 CARROT, PEELED AND DICED

2 GARLIC CLOVES, CHOPPED

5 SLICES OF PANCETTA, DICED

2 LARGE SPRIGS OF THYME

2 TABLESPOONS OLIVE OIL

25G UNSALTED BUTTER

1 MEDIUM BUTTERNUT SQUASH

3 RIPE WILLIAMS OR CONFERENCE PEARS

150G COOKED, PEELED CHESTNUTS

800ML HOT CHICKEN STOCK, PLUS EXTRA IF NEEDED

100ML DOUBLE CREAM

150G HUNGARIAN MANGALICA SPICED SALAMI OR CHORIZO, DICED

SALT AND FRESHLY GROUND BLACK PEPPER

Tip the onion, leek, celery, carrot, garlic and pancetta into a large pan. Add one of the thyme sprigs, 1 tablespoon of the olive oil and the butter. Cook over a low–medium heat for about 10 minutes until the veggies are tender but not coloured.

While they are cooking, peel, deseed and dice the squash, and peel, quarter, core and dice two of the pears.

Add the squash to the pan with the pears and 100g of the chestnuts and cook for a further 2–3 minutes. Pour in the stock and season well with salt and black pepper, then cover and bring to the boil. Reduce to a gentle simmer and cook for a about 30 minutes until the squash is tender when tested with the point of a knife.

Fish out the thyme sprig and blend the soup using a stick blender until smooth. Add the cream and a little more stock if the soup is on the thick side, then taste for seasoning, adding more salt and pepper as required.

Peel, core and dice the remaining pear and chestnuts. Heat the remaining 1 tablespoon of olive oil in a frying pan, add the salami or chorizo and cook until starting to brown. Throw in the pear, chestnuts and leaves from the remaining thyme sprig and cook for a further minute or so until the pear is tender and caramelised.

Ladle the soup into bowls, top with a good spoonful of the pear and salami/chorizo mixture and serve immediately.

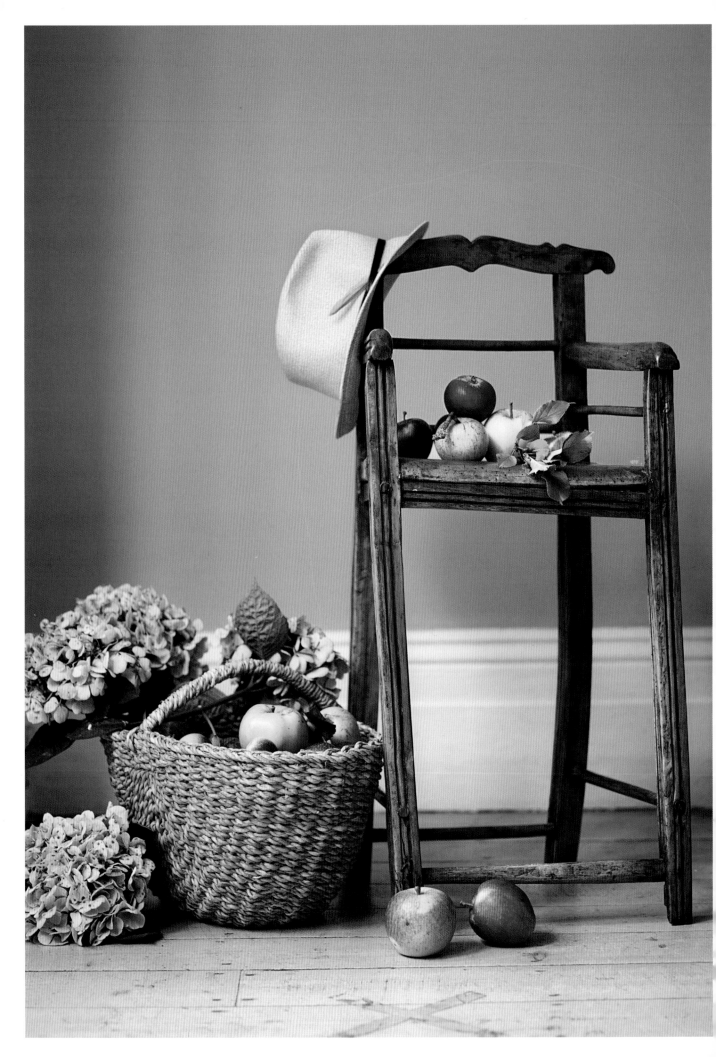

Orchard Fruit Galette

Galettes are the easiest fruit tarts to prepare, requiring no special tins or skills. This pastry uses a combination of plain and rye flours, which adds a nutty crispness, but you could also use spelt flour in place of rye if you prefer.

SERVES 6–8

For the pastry

200G PLAIN FLOUR, PLUS EXTRA FOR DUSTING

100G RYE FLOUR

A GOOD PINCH OF SEA SALT

200G UNSALTED BUTTER, CHILLED

40G HAZELNUTS, FINELY GROUND

40G CASTER SUGAR

3 TABLESPOONS ICED WATER

2 TEASPOONS CIDER VINEGAR OR LEMON
JUICE, PLUS EXTRA IF NEEDED

For the filling

JUICE OF 1 LEMON

100G CASTER SUGAR, PLUS 3 TABLESPOONS

3 SMALL QUINCES

3 CRISP APPLES, PEELED, QUARTERED AND
THINLY SLICED

3 RIPE PEARS, PEELED, QUARTERED AND
THINLY SLICED

½ TEASPOON GROUND CINNAMON

40G UNSALTED BUTTER

1 TABLESPOON MILK

To make the pastry, add the flours and salt to a large mixing bowl. Coarsely grate in the butter and, using a round-bladed knife, cut it into the flour, just so that it starts to be rubbed in. Then use your fingertips to lightly rub the butter into the flour, lifting the mixture up out of the bowl and letting it almost roll over your fingertips. You don't want to fully incorporate the butter – it should still be visible in the flour. Add the ground hazelnuts and sugar and lightly mix. Combine the iced water and vinegar or lemon juice in a cup and add almost all to the bowl. Mix, using the knife again, until the pastry starts to come together, adding more liquid if necessary. Gather the dough together, trying not to knead it, shape into a ball and flatten into a disc, then cover with clingfilm and chill for 2 hours.

Meanwhile, prepare the filling. Add 500ml of cold water, the lemon juice and 100g of sugar to a medium saucepan. Peel, quarter and core the quinces one at a time and immediately drop into the pan. Place over a medium heat and bring slowly to the boil to dissolve the sugar. Cover with a disc of baking parchment and simmer gently for about 25 minutes until tender. Leave to cool in the syrup.

Preheat the oven to 180°C/gas mark 4. Line a baking tray with parchment paper. Tip the apple and pear slices into a large bowl. Drain the quince from the cooking syrup, cut each quarter into slices and add to the bowl. Add 2 tablespoons of the sugar and the cinnamon and mix well.

Lightly dust the work surface with flour, roll out the pastry into a disc 2–3mm thick and place on the lined baking tray. Pile the fruit into the middle, leaving a border of 8cm all around, and dot with the butter. Fold the pastry up and around the fruit – don't worry too much about finesse for this tart. Brush the pastry with the milk and scatter with the remaining sugar. Bake on the middle shelf of the oven for 10 minutes, then reduce the temperature to 170°C/gas mark 3 and cook for a further 25–30 minutes until the pastry is golden and crisp and the fruit tender. Serve warm.

Quince and Almond Tart

In this recipe, poached and baked quinces are served alongside and in the middle of a rich almondy cake.

SERVES 8

JUICE OF 1 LEMON

100G CASTER SUGAR

4 SMALL QUINCES

50G UNSALTED BUTTER

125G CLEAR HONEY

2 TABLESPOONS MARSALA

1 SMALL CINNAMON STICK

2 BAY LEAVES

2 STRIPS OF ORANGE PEEL

2 STRIPS OF PEEL FROM AN UNWAXED LEMON

JUICE OF ½ ORANGE

For the shortbread base

125G PLAIN FLOUR

100G UNSALTED BUTTER, CHILLED AND DICED

40G ICING SUGAR, PLUS EXTRA FOR DUSTING

A PINCH OF SALT

For the cake mixture

4 LARGE EGGS, SEPARATED

175G CASTER SUGAR

FINELY GRATED ZEST OF 1 UNWAXED LEMON

½ TEASPOON GROUND CINNAMON

1 TEASPOON ORANGE FLOWER WATER

225G GROUND ALMONDS

A PINCH OF SALT

Equipment

21CM SPRINGFORM CAKE TIN

Pour 600ml of cold water into a medium saucepan and add the lemon juice and sugar. Peel and quarter the quinces one at a time and immediately drop into the pan – don't worry about removing the cores at this stage. Place over a medium heat and bring slowly to the boil to dissolve the sugar. Cover the fruit with a disc of baking parchment and simmer gently for about 25 minutes until tender.

Prepare the shortbread base. Preheat the oven to 180°C/gas mark 4 and line the base of the tin with baking parchment. Tip the flour, butter, icing sugar and salt into a food processor and pulse until the butter has been rubbed into the flour and the mixture starts to clump together. Tip the crumbly dough into the prepared tin and, using your hands, press into an even layer covering the base. Bake on the middle shelf of the oven for 12–15 minutes until pale golden.

Line a baking tin with baking parchment. Remove the quince quarters from the pan and arrange eight in the prepared tin, core-side uppermost. Dot with the butter, spoon over the honey and Marsala and tuck in the cinnamon stick, bay leaves and orange and lemon peels. Add the orange juice and 2 tablespoons of the quince poaching liquid. Cover loosely with another sheet of parchment and bake on the middle shelf of the oven for 40 minutes or until very soft when tested with the point of a sharp knife. Leave to cool in the tin.

Core and slice the remaining poached quinces and scatter over the shortbread base. To make the cake mixture, whisk the egg yolks and sugar until thick, pale and doubled in volume. Whisk in the lemon zest, cinnamon and orange flower water. Fold in the ground almonds. In another bowl, whisk the egg whites with the salt until they hold stiff peaks, then carefully fold into the almond mixture until there are no streaks of egg white remaining. Spoon the mixture on top of the quince, spread level and bake on the middle shelf for 40 minutes until golden brown, well risen and a skewer inserted into the middle comes out clean. Allow to cool in the tin. Serve the cake in slices, dusted with icing sugar, with the baked quinces.

Ham Hock and Pickled Quince Salad

Pickled quince will keep for weeks in the fridge and are a delicious accompaniment for cold cuts, the vinegary but aromatic fruit being especially good with ham. Try also adding them chopped to a stuffing for pork or lamb.

SERVES 6

1 HAM HOCK

1 ONION, QUARTERED

1 CARROT, ROUGHLY CHOPPED

1 CELERY STICK, ROUGHLY CHOPPED

1 BAY LEAF

1 SPRIG OF THYME

3–4 BLACK PEPPERCORNS

1 TABLESPOON DIJON MUSTARD

2 TABLESPOONS CLEAR HONEY

For the pickled quinces

550ML CIDER VINEGAR

400G GOLDEN CASTER SUGAR

4 CLOVES

3 JUNIPER BERRIES

4 BLACK PEPPERCORNS

1 STAR ANISE

1 CINNAMON STICK

1 BAY LEAF

2 STRIPS OF RIND FROM AN UNWAXED LEMON

4 QUINCES

To serve

75G WALNUTS

A BUNCH OF WATERCRESS

1 SMALL HEAD OF RADICCHIO, LEAVES SEPARATED

5 TABLESPOONS WALNUT OIL

2 TABLESPOONS CIDER VINEGAR

1 ROUNDED TEASPOON DIJON MUSTARD

2 TABLESPOONS ROUGHLY CHOPPED FLAT-LEAF PARSLEY

SALT AND FRESHLY GROUND BLACK PEPPER

Equipment

2 x 450G JAM JARS

Start by preparing the pickled quinces. Add all the ingredients, except the quinces, to a large stainless steel saucepan and bring slowly to the boil to dissolve the sugar. Simmer for 2 minutes, then remove from the heat. Leave for 30 minutes to allow the aromatics to flavour the vinegar.

As quinces discolour quickly, prepare one fruit at a time. Peel, quarter and core, then cut each quarter again in half or, depending on size, into thirds – aim for slices no more than 1cm thick. Immediately drop into the vinegar. Cover with a disc of baking parchment and bring the vinegar back to the boil, then simmer for 30 minutes or until the fruit is tender when pierced with the point of a sharp knife. Ladle into the warm sterilised jars (see page 132), seal tightly and leave until cold before labelling and storing in the fridge until needed.

Place the ham hock in a deep saucepan – you need one big enough to allow the ham to be submerged in water. Add the veggies, herbs and peppercorns, then cover the hock with cold water. Half cover the pan with a lid, bring to the boil over a medium heat, then simmer for 2–2½ hours until the meat is very tender and starting to pull away from the bone. Remove from the heat and leave to cool in the liquid. Drain the ham, reserving 200ml of the poaching liquid.

Preheat the oven to 190°C/gas mark 5. Line a roasting tin with a double thickness of foil.

Using a sharp knife, remove the skin from the ham hock, leaving a nice thick layer of fat, and stand upright in the lined roasting tin. Mix the mustard and honey together and slather it over the ham, then pour the reserved poaching liquid into the tin so that it comes no more than 1cm up the sides of the ham. Bake on the middle shelf for 30–40 minutes until well glazed, basting two or three times during cooking. Lightly toast the walnuts on a baking tray while the oven is on, then leave the ham and nuts to cool.

Tip the watercress and radicchio into a large bowl. Place the oil, vinegar and mustard in a jam jar, season well, screw on the lid and shake well. Toss the salad leaves with enough dressing to coat, arrange on serving plates and scatter with the toasted walnuts. Shred the ham into small bite-sized pieces and add to the salad. Finally, drain about 4 pickled quince slices per person and arrange on top. Scatter with the parsley and serve.

Index

Acknowledgements

Writing a book is never the work of just one person – there's a whole team of brilliantly talented people involved, without whom it would just be a jumble of words.

I feel incredibly lucky to write for Kyle Books, and can't thank Kyle enough for asking me to write another book – it seems a very long time ago that we had lunch at my kitchen table discussing this. My editor Judith Hannam really is one of the best and I thank my lucky stars every day that I get to work with her. Thank you for being so patient when my deadline was 'looming' and when I went silent during my house move. And for indulging me yet again, with pages that are chock full of beautiful pictures, for putting together such a fantastic team and for pulling everything together in your unflappable and gentle manner. Thank you also to Hannah Coughlin and Corinne Masciocchi for your meticulous double checking and proof-reading – eagle eyed the pair of you.

Yet again I have had the absolute pleasure to work with my great friend and brilliant photographer Tara Fisher. What you have bought to this book is beyond words. I have loved working with you for a few days at a time, every month for the 12 months that we worked on the photography – thank you my friend. Thank you to the best-set painter in town – Ms Saskia Sierra – your choice of colours was spot on! And to Ms Liliana Sierra who stood holding ice creams so perfectly for what must have felt like an eternity before we allowed her to actually eat one. And thanks to Sue Prescott for your brilliant re-touching and for keeping us sane and laughing.

To my wonderful assistant Kathryn Bruton, who is so much more than an assistant, you're a true friend, wonderful talent and undisputed Queen of Soda Bread.

Miranda Harvey, whose incredibly beautiful design for this book really has bowled me over.

Mr Mungo Jerry Boogaloo, who is getting increasingly stubborn with old age but thankfully will still accompany me on a good walk every day, just so long as we're going the way he wants to go and I have a pocket full of treats.

And finally to Hughie – thank you thank you thank you. *x*